Till Death Us Do Part?

TILL DEATH US DO PART?

Sue Ashdown

eagle

Guildford, Surrey

Copyright © 1998 Sue Ashdown

The rights of Sue Ashdown to be identified as author of this work has been asserted by her in accordance with the Copyright, Design and Patents Act 1988.

British Library Cataloguing in Publication Data. A catalogue record for this book is available from the British Library.

Published by Eagle, an imprint of Inter Publishing Service (IPS) Ltd, St Nicholas House, 14 The Mount, Guildford, Surrey GU2 5HN.

Scriptures quoted from The Good News Bible, published by The Bible Societies/Harper Collins Ltd., UK American Bible Society, 1966, 1971, 1976, 1992, 1994.

Typeset by Eagle Publishing
Printed by Cox & Wyman, Reading
ISBN No: 0 86347 257 5

CONTENTS

	Foreword	7
	Preface	11
1	In the Beginning . . .	13
2	Betrayal and Rejection	31
3	Expectations and Response	45
4	Feelings Christians 'Shouldn't' Have (I) Guilt – the Christian Dilemma	58
5	Feelings Christians 'Shouldn't' Have (II) Anger and Fear	75
6	Feelings Christians 'Shouldn't' Have (III) Anxiety and Doubt	89
7	Feelings Christians 'Shouldn't' Have (IV) Despair – A Pain Beyond Bereavement	106
8	Divorce – The Decree Absolute	119
9	Other People's Stories (I) – Brenda	135
10	Other People's Stories (II) – Christine	147
11	Other People's Stories (III) – Elizabeth	158
12	Other People's Stories (IV) – Robert	170
13	Acceptance and Forgiveness?	180
14	Peeping Out – Learning to Live Again	197
15	Reality – An Unshakeable God	214
	Appendix 1	235
	Bibliography	238
	List of Help Agencies	239

This book is dedicated to two very special people – my daughters – Jenny and Sally. Without their unconditional love and constant support I would not have made it through this far. Their love warms my heart and their laughter lights up my life.

FOREWORD

by Jennifer Rees Larcombe

For ages you may have been searching in vain for a book like this, if 'the person you love most in the whole world has suddenly changed their perception of you,' or if you have friends or family whose marriages are breaking apart and you simply don't know what to say or how to help. There are shelves full of Christian books on how to have a good marriage but sometimes, however many we read, a Christian marriage fails. Until now, it was extremely difficult to find a readable, common-sense book to help us through the agony.

In my opinion this book stands in a class of its own, amongst Christian books, for a number of reasons. Many of them are written by people who have had an experience which needs to be communicated but, although they may be wonderful Christians, they are not necessarily good writers. Sue not only has a story to tell but she also has the skill to tell it brilliantly.

Her book, however, is far more than just an absorbing story; it is a unique blend of practical common-sense advice, earthy humour and deep spirituality. She not only draws from her own experience but uses and contrasts the experience of four other very different people, which gives this book a most unusual dimension. Two of them are close friends of mine, so I can fully appreciate how well Sue has captured the essence of their experiences and handed them to us in such a readable form.

Sue's 'scribblings' (the highly inappropriate way she describes her beautiful poems) form another aspect which makes this book delightfully different. They come straight from her spirit which, like a rose, has been crushed to release the full sweetness of its fragrance. Sue's poetry blends in amongst the text and is used like exquisitely drawn word pictures to illustrate the way she feels.

However, the main thing which puts this book head and shoulders above many Christian books is its stark reality and total honesty.

Sue tells it how it is. Perhaps many Christian authors write their books too long after the experiences they describe. They have worked through all the painful negative feelings and been so successful in letting them go that they have forgotten they ever existed. Sue wrote her book while her wounds were still open and raw, and when you happen to be in the same state yourself you appreciate that! It all feels worse when you read about others who are so much further along the road to wholeness that they seem to be looking back in exasperation at the slowness of your progress. Sue seems to be walking beside us, feeling with us and even helping us to laugh a little at our fumbling, stumbling frailty.

I have to admit that my hair stood on end a bit when I first read her chapter on forgiveness. 'Sue! You can't *say* that,' I said out aloud. 'Lots of us think like that but as Christians we can't admit it – let alone say it in print!' Then I read the chapter again and realised I had totally misunderstood her point. So, if that chapter makes you prickle too, read it through again prayerfully before you write her a nasty letter! Her poem on the agony of trying to forgive is sublime and will prove, for many, both refreshing and liberating.

When Sue told me she felt God wanted her to write her story my first reaction was pure joy. My own marriage had recently broken down, so I knew just how badly her book was needed by a rapidly growing number of wounded Christians. However, I also knew just how much time and energy a book takes to write, and nursing at a Christian Healing Centre already absorbs most of her available time. Most of all, I know only too well how painful it is to relive past events through writing about them, and how vulnerable you feel when you expose your most intimate feelings to others so publicly. Yet, in spite of all that, Sue has managed it, and I can only think that God must have had a lot to do with it!

Reading the manuscript during this last week has been a deeply moving experience for me; painful but profoundly healing. I would like to be the first of many to thank Sue for being both brave and generous enough to give us this special gift of herself.

Jennifer Rees Larcombe
Hadlow, March 1998.

My Lord of Round-The-Corner

The precipice is narrow
And the sides are very steep –
The bottom is deep – and dark – and far away.
Ahead is darkness
And I can see no hands to lead me on –
And it's hard to walk carrying a cross.
If I could see with my Father's eyes
I would see a bend in the path –
I would see round the corner
To where Jesus stands,
Arms reaching out.
He is my "Lord of round-the-corner" –
For my God is God of the darkness
As well as the light.

But for now I walk with the blind eyes of faith
Along the precipice –
Knowing only that my Father uses
As a rope to keep me from falling
My honesty in saying that I cannot see the way
ahead.

PREFACE

I hope this is an honest book. It is written for people who want or need to be honest, but who feel lonely, maybe frightened, certainly confused, and always terribly, desperately hurt.

Because of the subject mater in the book, some names and places have been changed to assure anonymity.

In Christian circles often so many masks are worn, and 'Christianspeak' abounds. It is frighteningly easy for us to slip into suffering from the Christian killer heart condition, 'hardening of the oughteries'. The prognosis, if the condition is left unchecked, is poor – death of reality, sometimes loss of compassion and almost certainly sublimation or denial of our true feelings. We become complacent in our cosy Christian worlds. Then for some of us, an event of such earth-shattering magnitude happens that our whole world is smashed and lies broken in little pieces around our feet. It is not just one tragic event, but what at the time feels like a cosmic disaster of epic proportions, involving every single part of our lives, both now and in the future.

Marriage breakdown is such an event. For Christians it gives rise not only to all the anguish and pain everyone experiences at this time, but it makes us question so many other things as well. For some, it causes a major crisis or even loss of faith. For others it brings a confusing cacophony of feelings which can leave us wondering if we are emotional and spiritual schizophrenics. This is not helped at all by the fact that for all of us, like Job, there are well-intentioned onlook-

11

ers who think they know so much better than we do how we should act, speak, live, and even feel! We are encouraged to hurry our healing, when deep inside we feel that complete healing may only come when we meet our God face to face. God never hurries us – He simply looks at us with love and total understanding and very deep compassion, saying: 'Take all the time you need to heal, My child, for I have all eternity to wait for you,' and then He smiles deep into our pain.

I have tried to write as honestly as I know how. I have certainly written from the heart. As you read the following pages, my hope and prayer, from my heart to yours, is this: That you will know, wherever you are on your own particular journey, that truly you are not alone.

I would like to say a big 'Thank you' to all those who have helped me to bring this book 'to birth'. Without their constant encouragement and support it would not have been born.

To my 'three J's'! Joyce, Jen, and Julie for their love, affirmation and prayers; Jackie for being my sister; Linda for being a star; Mary and her brown Micra; Tony and Shirley for standing with me; Zoë for being an angel; Martin and Ann for cups of coffee and sanity; Janie for understanding; Jackie, Jo and Nick for clever typing; Fr James for walking beside me; Cath for believing in me; my colleagues at Burrswood for love, prayers, laughter and hugs, and for all those friends who have prayed me through every line.

Sue Ashdown

Chapter One

IN THE BEGINNING

My husband's voice rang out, young and strong, across the crowded church.

'With this ring I thee wed . . . With my body I thee worship . . . In sickness and in health, for richer for poorer . . . For better for worse, till death us do part . . .'

As he spoke he turned to look at me and smiled. I smiled back through my veil of fine white net and through eyes misty with tears of happiness. He was every young woman's dream – tall, dark and very, very handsome! We were full of hopes and dreams, standing on the threshold of life as we took our vows that day – thirty long and eventful years ago. He was about to be ordained as an Anglican clergyman and we looked forward to a future of serving God in parish ministry. We were young, we were in love and life, it seemed, waited for us with open arms – exciting, challenging, full of promise – and we were so ready to embrace it and live it to the full. But most of all on that September day, as we stood side by side in the lovely church filled with friends, families and flowers, we were together.

How could I have known, on that warm late summer's afternoon, that one terrible, frightening day far into the future, those vows which rang out so clear and true would be broken, snapped in two, and my life, which was then so full of hope, would lie in tatters at my feet, smashed and torn? How could I have guesed, as the wide gold band was slipped on to my finger, that it would later imprison me inside a life so filled with pain and grief that I would feel as if I stood on the very edge of madness? If we could look into the future, I do not think we would do it, for we learn mostly by our mistakes. Life would not be life if we could see what was round every corner. True, there would be no shocks, but there would be no surprises either, and life would lose that spontaneity of joy – those sudden happinesses which are the more acute precisely because they are unexpected. Would I have done anything differently if I could have known what was to happen? As the story unfolds, I hope my answer becomes clear.

But on that September day, as we walked together out of the church into the late afternoon sun, with all the untouched hopefulness of youth, I was walking into what for me was a dream come true. The man I loved so much was by my side and I thought it would be ever thus. How wrong I was.

The year in Cambridge while my husband completed his theological training was a very happy one, and passed incredibly quickly.

This was followed by his ordination and a curacy in West Yorkshire, where our first daughter was born. It was a happy start to the ordained ministry and life as a 'clergy couple'. The vicar and his wife in charge of the large and busy parish were a fantastic pair, and we both learned much from them. We found that we really loved Yorkshire and when we left that first parish after three years, I knew that one day we both hoped very much to return to that part of the world.

Then came a second curacy of three years in Northamptonshire. We lived in a tiny modern house on a large housing estate, and it was whilst there that our second daughter was born. We were very fortunate in that we again had a lovely couple in our vicar and his wife. These were three really happy years and some of the friends we made there we have kept ever since.

Then it was time for my husband to take on an

incumbency. I can still remember the day a letter came from the Provost of a city in West Yorkshire, asking if we would like to look at a parish there with a view to my husband becoming the rector. I can clearly remember us grabbing each other's hands in the kitchen and jumping up and down with glee at the prospect! I felt like writing back and saying: 'Do we want to look at it? Is the Pope catholic . . .?!' How could I have known, as we literally danced round our kitchen together with joy, that by accepting that parish it would mean the beginning of several very happy years – but also set our feet on a road that would eventually lead to unimaginable suffering?

And so we moved back 'up North' and there followed eight of the happiest and most fulfilled years of my life. Quite simply, we loved it. We loved the people, the place, the whole pace of life, and after coming from the 'deep South' the open-hearted and honest friendship of the Northerners delighted us. They said we had to be there for fifty years before becoming locals! So we remained 'off-comedens' – but they treated us with great friendship even so. I think they would have been quite happy for us to remain there for the full fifty years and certainly we would have been – by then both our girls had broad Yorkshire accents – lovely!

It was whilst here that with the beauty of the Northern dales and moors around me I began to 'scribble' – to write my thoughts and feelings down, only they seemed to come out as poetry!

But there comes a time in parish ministry when you just know it is time to move on. It was a very real wrench and with great sadness that we left the church in that really lovely Northern village. I remember my elder daughter running across the kitchen, bursting into tears and throwing herself into my arms because she had just said goodbye to her best friend. My heart wept for her and as I held her I silently pleaded with God to keep and protect her and her sister in our new town. It is not easy to leave a much-loved parish and move on.

My mother had died whilst we were up North. She was not old, but my husband's parents were getting elderly and we moved back to the South to be near our relatives. That first day walking through the new town, my heart yearned for the friendly Northerners we had left behind and I wondered if I would ever be happy again. We had left some very firm friendships back up North.

However, we rapidly got to know people in our new church and town, and they welcomed us very warmly. Then followed five very happy and fulfilling years. It was a busy and active church, and I enjoyed it enormously. Again deep friendships were formed which continue to this day, and I still visit my friends there as they do me.

Parish life was always hectically busy for both of us. A huge vicarage with a beautiful garden, both needing lots of time and care. Two school-age children. The demands on the home – prayer meetings, young wives' groups, home groups, committee meetings, singing and music group practices, sacred dance practices, parish concert practices – practices of every kind, it seemed! Then there were the people who came seeking help and comfort with many and varied problems and unhappinesses. People to be visited, coffee mornings, youth clubs, pathfinders – the list was endless, all topped off with the never-ending utterly relentless phone calls! But I *loved* it all. Sure there were times I longed not only to unplug our phone but vandalise it too so it would never work again! But I enjoyed parish life enormously, and at our local 'clergy wives' meetings' I got one or two very odd looks for openly saying how much I loved being 'a vicar's wife'!

Whilst in this parish, I felt called to become an Oblate of St Benedict, joining a large Benedictine community relatively nearby. A Benedictine Oblate is called to live life according to the rule of St Benedict. In this case, it means living the contemplative life outside of the cloister, which is a special way of living a life of prayer in our everyday lives. It is a vocation, or call, from God, but it does not involve becoming a professed nun or monk. Oblates can be single, married, men or women. It is a commitment which is taken on for life, although we renew our promises yearly. This commitment involves following a 'Rule of life' which is lived out in a number of ways – including visits to the Abbey, and being linked with an individual 'Oblate Sister', with whom we meet at prearranged times. (see Appendix). This was, and still is, a source of indescribable joy to me and proved to be a rock of stability and support for the years about to come. The love of the community and their prayers, the discipline of saying the Divine Office, the beauty of the place itself, and at least *trying* to live the contemplative life: all this has held me through the storms which did, and still do, happen in my life.

As we served and lived in that place, little did I know that the storm-clouds were gathering over our busy vicarage and lives. Little did I know that just as the great storms were preparing to sweep the South, ripping up trees, damaging buildings, causing chaos and destruction, so in *my* life and that of my daughters, and indeed the whole parish, dark forces were working to wreak havoc and unbelievable destruction and death. Little did I know that soon this happy, hectic, fulfilling life was to be snatched away from me and I would be torn from that vicarage and parish just as surely as the trees were torn from the earth and knocked to the ground. How could I guess that soon, like the trees, I would be lying torn and dying on the ground, as unable as they to stand upright again?

True, I did see the signs. An overfriendliness with a member of my healing prayer group (and yes, I *know* all prayer is healing, but this one met in the vicarage to pray specifically for the healing of hurts and dis-eases). I noticed times when my husband took much longer to do certain things. He was out much longer than usual on visits. He kept going for 'walks'. All sorts of little pointers. He appeared to be distracted and offhand at times, as though he were some place else. It seemed to me that he was becoming very unhappy.

It would be quite wrong to describe in detail all that happened in the next months, but eventually we came to a Monday morning and I asked my husband, not for the first time, what on earth was the matter. I thought maybe he was having a crisis of faith, or was feeling 'burnt out'. At the time we were trying to plan a holi-day, but I found him evasive and rather offhand about it all. I remember reminding him that he had denied having an affair and asking him please to tell me what was wrong and stop saying 'nothing'.

With two short words, he destroyed my life. He said: 'I lied' – and I knew immediately what he had lied about and with whom.

At that moment something inside me went 'click' like a light going out, which in a way, it had. Something in me died – it was not my love for him, for that has never dimmed. Would that it had, for the next years would then have been so much easier. I was left in darkness with all my certainties and securities stripped away – ripped from me. I felt naked, vulnera-ble, alone and very, very frightened.

When a clergyman commits adultery and resigns his living, a dreadful machinery goes into motion. I will always remember the day of my husband's resignation. The Archdeacon brought the forms to the vicarage and we all sat in the lounge. As my husband signed the forms, the Archdeacon held my gaze, willing me to be strong, for he and I both knew that in a matter of days I would be alone with my daughters as my husband left the house and went to live with 'the other woman'. I did not understand it then, and I do not understand it now. How can any woman, saying she loves a man, allow him to give up something so precious as the priesthood? It is totally unlike resigning from an ordinary job or profession. It is part of what makes the priest the very person he or she is. By forcing them to choose between the priesthood and themselves, they actually destroy a large part of the person they profess to love. I once heard it said by a Bishop that 'loving is seeing with the eyes of those it loves'. How true that is. I suppose *they* would say: 'Well, I am seeing with his eyes. What he really wants is *me*.' But that, I think, is a delusion. For how can it be true, unselfish love which tears a clergyman away from his calling, urges him to abandon his wife and his daughters who need their father, rips a parish apart, and brings shame to the very name of the God he serves? To my mind, real love would break off the relationship and leave him where he has chosen and committed himself to be. For a priest it is not just giving up his job – it is giving up *everything*, including that large part of himself which is consecrated to the priesthood. Technically, my husband remains in Holy Orders, but is forbidden to celebrate as a priest. That, to me, is hardly living, as I heard quoted in a sermon at a friend's priesting, as 'a priest forever, after the order of Melchizedek' (Psalm 110 verse 4).

In the weeks that followed it seemed that every time I answered the door the Bishop and Archdeacon were standing there! There was so much to sort out. I had two heart-broken and confused children to love and care for, and I wanted to give them the time they needed to try and cope. The press got hold of the story and I had the *Daily This* and the *Daily That*, plus all the local rags, on the phone wanting all the gory details. Friends and I phoned everyone whose name was in the parish magazine asking them to say nothing to any of the media. Dreadful though it was to see our names across the front pages, I took silent satisfaction that they had very few facts to print. Like everything else, for them it was a nine-day wonder, but for us it was ghastly while it lasted.

The Archdeacon explained that the Church would buy a house and I could rent it. I had to choose which house and where. Obviously I had to stay in the area because of my girls' schooling. They had had more than enough disruption and needed at least some stability in their lives. Unfortunately, it was at a time when houses were selling before the details could even be typed and I had to phone several estate agents every day. Difficult to believe now! It was my younger daughter who actually found an ad in the paper for the house we eventually moved into. We all loved it from the first moment we saw it, even though every inch needed re-decorating – but an army of helpers, both family and friends, got it ready just in time. All this was done whilst I sorted and packed up our huge vicarage, looked for a full-time job to support us and tried to sort out the chaos in the parish which a shock resignation brings. I was permanently exhausted and it was only the support of family and friends that kept me going. I will say more later about this support, or in some cases lack of it, how I had some lovely surprises and some very nasty shocks indeed.

I clung to God like a drowning person and He clung on to me for dear life. We clung together, and even though at times, through exhaustion, confusion and grief, He seemed rather misty, I knew with everything in me that He was always there. I had, of course, to find a new church, and because of the sensitivity of the situation, one away from where we lived. I was really fortunate in finding a super, very high Anglo-Catholic church six miles from us, where both priest and people welcomed me very warmly. Father Timothy was kindness and compassion itself and a great source of help to me. I loved being in my new church enormously and enjoyed the worship more than I can say. There were many times when Father Timothy's shoulder was a great comfort, and with his down-to-earth and sensitive counsel he saw me through many a bad day. He was large in both body and spirit and whenever I saw him I felt safe and knew he truly understood my pain.

We loved our new little house and life slowly and painfully took on a new 'normality'. I worked at the Church of England's healing centre six miles away and loved it from the first day. I was able to be home when my girls arrived back from school. By this time they were teenagers and we helped each other through the bad times and grew into a closeness which has remained to this day and I know is very, very special.

After a year, my husband asked if he could return to us. I was overjoyed. I am a firm believer in second chances, and so we three girls prepared for my husband to return. He and I planned to re-take our marriage vows with my spiritual director, a priest we both loved and respected, on a Friday, and then take the girls on a week's holiday on the Isle of Wight. I am sure it is not difficult to imagine my horror, on returning home on the Wednesday, two days before the service, to have my husband tell me it was all a ghastly mistake – he 'could not live a lie' and was going back to the other woman. There are simply no words, either in poetry or prose, to describe my feelings that night. Sufficient to say I felt as though I were in hell.

The girls and I went, with my older daughter's boyfriend, to the Isle of Wight and, incredibly, had a good holiday. I just had to try not to think too hard about the past, or indeed the now, once again, very frightening future. I think it was in that week that I started to learn a very important lesson. I began to learn to 'live for the day'. The past was far too painful and the future simply too terrifying and uncertain. 'The sacrament of the present moment' has truly been one of my lifesavers, both then and now.

I had to face the simple truth, that my husband truly did not want me. After much thought and prayer, I decided that my final gift to him would be his freedom and I commenced divorce proceedings. It took nearly another year and many painful decisions and difficult periods until I found myself one day waiting to go into the town where we lived. The decree nisi had been granted and the decree absolute was due any day. I was suddenly convinced, overwhelmingly, that in town that day I would bump into my husband and that it mattered that I did. So strong was the conviction that I even changed into what I knew was his favourite dress! I *did* bump into him and as a result of that meeting in a local coffee shop he *did* come back. We re-took our marriage vows with Bishop Peter in a simple and moving ceremony.

I remember the day my husband actually returned to me. We stood in the kitchen of our little house. He took me in his arms and said: 'I've come back, Susie, and I'll never leave you again.' I was so happy – it was a dream come true. I believed him with my whole heart. I wanted to, so I did.

Then followed a very happy year while we lived as a 'normal' couple. He continued in his secular job and I in mine and we revelled in being a family again. The girls were so happy to have the father they loved back home and the times we spent as a family were very precious and cherished by us all. There was only one thing missing – the priesthood. Within that year my husband was allowed to help Father Timothy in the church he now attended with me. I remember how overjoyed he was to be back celebrating the Eucharist. He said it 'felt so good' and I could see and sense how right it was. Pastorally he was excellent and very popular and he still remains to me one of the best and clearest preachers I have ever heard.

At the end of another year, he was instituted as the priest in charge of a daughter church. Cliff and Sylvia, the rector and his wife in charge of the main parish church, were a wonderful couple, full of fun and lightness, but with a deep faith too. They both had very caring natures and I never once felt that they had become bogged down by the job. When we four were all together, there was much craziness and often much helpless laughter too! I loved that parish. The people were friendly. We had a super church house, which both the girls loved coming home to when their nursing careers in London allowed. We made good friends there and we both loved it. It was so good to be back together, even better to be ministering together once again. I often used to think that God was smiling as He saw us together.

I am aware that some people reading this may say: 'How stupid she was, how blind! *Surely* she could tell something was wrong. She *must* have been able to tell.' I am thought by many of my friends, and my husband, to be an intuitive person. But *this* I did not know. It is the one thing that always happens to other people – never you. I just enjoyed us being together, as I believed we were meant to be.

It was not until late summer of that final year that I again knew something was wrong with my husband. Once again, whenever I gently asked him: 'What's wrong?' he always answered as before: 'Nothing.' And that was all he would ever say. He suggested we go to Israel to celebrate our Silver Wedding. I love the Holy Land, and readily agreed. It was during that pilgrimage that I knew that something was terribly wrong. The holiday was ruined for me, for I felt that he was distracted, distant and offhand, and I was very hurt by his attitude to me. Even the leader of our party asked me what his problem was, but with only 'nothing' to go on, I had nothing to prepare me for the terrible twist in my life that was just around the corner. When someone constantly denies anything is wrong and you know full well something *is*, there is very little you can *do* about it. There was a lack of honesty, concern was called 'nagging' and the coin finally flipped over fully when the refrain became 'Nothing is wrong except you constantly asking me what is wrong', so I began to take the blame for his obvious preoccupation with something else. He did not appear to be unhappy. We still, as always, laughed and had fun together, but something was draining the very life out of him and I had no idea what it was, and even less that it was not a 'what' but a 'who' which was tearing him apart and causing him such unhappiness. Whatever it was, I wanted to stamp it out and help him find again his peace of mind.

It was shortly before Christmas when the final curtain rose on the drama of our life together. I was having a lie-in prior to a late start in my part-time job, and I was sitting in bed enjoying the cup of tea my husband had brought me. I was looking forward to the girls coming home for Christmas and felt very happy and contented. I was opening a big pile of Christmas cards when I came across a typed envelope from a large northern city close to the lovely little village where we had spent so many happy years. I was puzzled because my friends up north usually wrote to me, not typed, but as I opened it I realised with a sickening lurch that it was not from a friend. It was from a member of the young wives' group I ran in that much-loved northern village. If anyone were to ask me if I have ever stared evil in the face, I would reply: 'Yes, and it happened in the shape of a letter.' The letter claimed that its writer and my husband had been 'seeing each other' for the past *eighteen* years. (I should explain here that this woman was not the same one with whom my husband had lived for two years after he left me three years before.) The letter also said that if I loved him I would 'give him up, or if you can't do that, share him'. Then it said several more things and ended by telling me that whatever *my* decision was they would 'continue seeing each other *as the need arose*'. My overriding emotion was shock, but also anger that such blatant selfishness could be penned in such a missive of destruction. I knew immediately that just like the first time this was not love but selfish desire, or else it would have put the needs of the beloved first and not its own. I experienced a dreadful feeling of *déjà vu*. Quite calmly, though shaking uncontrollably, I walked downstairs to where my husband was reading the newspaper and equally as calmly swore at him as I showed him the letter.

What can I say about the next months? All the same initial numbness and then the same searing agony. Three people kept me sane. The first was my G.P. who was a really lovely Christian doctor – I just knew he felt my pain. He did not pretend to know the answers – there were none. He did not pretend even to know what to say – he was just there every time I needed him. He wept with me and did something not many people *can* do – he entered the depths of my agony and rejection with me – and he stayed. He was never embarrassed nor hasty. He stayed with me when I was lost and trying to stay alive, whilst wounds I thought had healed were ripped open again and bled. He and I both knew that this time, because of the scar tissue, they would take so much longer even to begin to heal.

The other two people who kept me alive were Cliff and Sylvia. It would be difficult to express in words either the depth of their compassion or the depth of my gratitude to them. Many times in those months I drove down to the vicarage and the door was *always* open for me. I used to just collapse on to Cliff's study floor and Sylvia held me through bouts of uncontrollable weeping while Cliff hovered in a concerned way in the background, but eventually when I could speak, they both listened to me as I poured out my grief and confusion, and they gave measured, sensitive and wise counsel. They helped me in so many different ways. People like them are rare and I consider myself very fortunate indeed to have them as my friends. As ever, and indeed most necessary for survival, humour reared its head and even if the cause was black indeed, I remember we found time not only to weep but to laugh too.

Telling my daughters was excruciating. I met them in the nurses' home in London. My stepmother came with me to help me, for I have only one pair of arms and I knew that on that day I would need two.

So, another resignation, and for the second time in my life I found myself packing up a church house. Dismantling our home, selling bits of it to friends and strangers alike, putting other bits in storage. On the final day of our married life, Cliff drove me to my sister's house in the town where I now live. I felt dead inside, and terribly, frighteningly tired. My sister was a rock, and still is. Always there, putting up with my snappy moments, cooking me meals when otherwise I would not have eaten, giving me lifts and all the time loving me. She is my best friend as well as my sister and without her I would have drowned, for I felt truly like I imagine a drowning person feels. For a start, this time I was truly alone. The girls were both nursing in London. I had no home, no church, no money, no job, no role, no town, no identity and no husband. My daughters were fantastic. At a time when their own grief must have been enormous, they constantly showed their love for me in many and different ways. They treated me with great tenderness and yet they were down-to-earth. They rang, they wrote, they visited. Without them my world, if it were possible, would have been an even darker place in which to be.

I felt as though I were in a very rough sea. There was no firmness under my feet. I was out of my depth in an alien and foreign environment, smashed ceaselessly against the rocks and never able to reach the shore. Waves crashed relentlessly over me and every time I felt firm ground I was dragged back out to the cold and dangerous depths. I thought indeed that I would drown and desperately tried to hold my hand above the waves so that God could hold it tight; I need not have worried for His other hand was in the water beneath me and He never once let me go. Even when I was too weak to hold on and I *did* let go, He gathered me in His arms and held me tight.

At this time I used to talk to Bishop Lindsay Urwin. He was, and still is, incredibly understanding and he helps me enormously. He said four words to me which have helped me more than anything else. No clichés, no out-of-context Bible verses, no trite easy answers, no platitudes. He said: 'Go with the flow.' Then he added: 'On the days that you feel happy, enjoy it, and on the days that you feel down, just go with it – don't fight.'

So, slowly and painfully, I stared to build up a new life. Sometimes it was two steps forward and one step back! Caring friends bought me a car. Eventually, with my sister's help, I found a flat and I got a full-time job in a convent. After 'shopping around', I found a new church, where I have been fortunate in making many good friends.

Again the vicar and his wife at my new church are a superb couple, loving and caring – no clichés, just letting me tell it how it is – and this time a bonus, a lovely lady curate, whose deep understanding and compassion helped me so many, many times. Her greatest gift to me, beside her friendship, was simply letting me be *me* and not arguing with me about who I was. This must have been very difficult for her as I did not know myself who I was – I still don't some days!

It is five years since my husband left me for the last time, and on bad days it still only feels like five hours. After thirty years of marriage, it is a long and winding road back to any kind of 'normality'. It cannot be 'got over' in a few years – healing does not come with a few tears and a quick prayer. We cannot try to 'forget' or 'rise above' the pain. We cannot and must not try to forget our pain in meeting the needs of others. That is only putting off facing and working through even a little of our own pain. We have to travel the road through it at our *own* speed, not other people's, however sincere they may be – but more of that later.

I have told my story in some detail. I have done this because I want you to know that I do not write from theories or ideas, but from experience of the problems. I know what it feels like to be betrayed by the one you love. I know how it feels to be abandoned – not once, but three times. I know what it is like to try and deal with what sometimes feels like intractable emotional pain. I know what it is like to be unable to stop loving the person who is responsible for that pain. That is why I have written my story and my sometimes random thoughts about Christian marriage breakdown. If it helps even one person who is in that deep place of confusion and fear, then it will have been worth it. You may tune in to what I say. For some the order of events and emotions may well be different. There *are* no rules. But there is always heartache, anger, fear, doubt, anxiety, confusion, sometimes despair. I give no definitive solutions because in such complex situations there are none. It is for each person to find their own way through, but there may well be little pointers on the way.

When it happened to me, each time I had a great need to see something written down about it all. I needed to see in print that these overwhelming emotions I was feeling were 'normal', were 'allowed', and that it was *all right* to feel them. I badly needed to know that I was not alone in the pain and confusion. I *knew* God was in my life. I wanted to believe He was in control but the evidence pointed otherwise. It did not *feel* as if He was in control, although I knew in my head that He was. I was a vicar's wife of twenty-nine years and a deeply committed Christian. I am a Benedictine Oblate. I love God with all my heart, and through it all I knew He loved me with a deep and never-ending love. I knew *all* this, but as I stood in the empty vicarage on that bleak winter's day I was honest enough to admit that even knowing all this I was a girl in trouble – deep trouble. I knew I needed help, support and comfort. I desperately wanted some answers, and if I could not find them, then I needed help to learn to live with the questions. I offer no answers, rather I address the problems. The German poet Rilke wrote[1]: 'Be patient towards all that is unresolved in your heart. Try to love the questions themselves. Do not seek the answers because you would not be able to live them. Live the questions now. Perhaps you will then, gradually, without noticing it, live some day into the answers.' I think the only answer I do offer is both a very simple and a very complex one. Ultimately it is the source of all our hopes, our dreams and our meaning for living. Quite simply, it is God. We can leave our past with Him, we can live the present with His help and we can trust the future to His care (Psalm 147, verses 3 and 5).

But He knows we have to get through each day. He knows and understands the depths of our pain. On those days when He seems distant, hang in there. When He feels near, enjoy. As Bishop Lindsay says, 'go with the flow'. Then we may, as Rilke wrote, 'live some day into the answers'.

I wrote the following poem just before I moved out of the vicarage the first time. I sat in our dining/music room where so many happy singing group practices had been held, where my daughters had practised the piano, recorders, guitar and clarinet. I sat in that room where so much had happened, and I wept. Outside it was pouring with rain. I have always loved roses, and as I looked through the window to the rosebeds outside, I saw that the roses were wet, battered and bowed. It suddenly struck me that they and I were very, very similar.

'Lord, It's Raining So Hard . . .'

Lord, it's raining so hard
And it looks as tho' the roses are weeping too
– As I weep

It looks as tho' their life's blood is slowly
Draining to the ground
– As mine is

Yes Lord, they still grow straight and tall,
But some are leaning a little –
Bowed under the weight of what is falling on them
– As I am

Their leaves will fall
They will be cut off and discarded –
Their flowers will be shattered this fall
– As I will be

But come the summer
When the sun shines again
– As it will
Their buds will appear,
Their perfume will return,
They will grow and be whole and lovely once again
– As I will be – as I will be

Chapter Two

BETRAYAL AND REJECTION

Offering
Whatever You would ask of me
O Lord Christ
Take

For in the asking is the taking
And in the giving
I receive

I stood in the middle of my lounge feeling confused and afraid. Could I face going to church? Could I face all those people? They would smile and greet me, and I would have to smile back, and to the inevitable 'Hallo Sue, how are you?', I would make the obligatory standard reply 'Oh, fine thanks.' If I were to say how I *really* felt, it would be: 'Actually John/Mary/Dave/Jean, I'm breaking up inside. I hurt so badly, I want to run away – so please just leave me alone.' But obviously I could not do that.

This is how betrayal and rejection can make us feel. We may *want* to go to church – we may want to simply sit in God's presence. Maybe actually to worship Him feels a tall order at that moment, but we want God, and we want to be in His house. For me, I wanted to make my Communion. It would be all right if we could creep in, sit in a pew and be invisible. To have to actually relate to another person, is too painful, too risky. To have a conversation with someone is to start, or continue, a relationship, and that involves the fear of being rejected again. The wounds we have are still bleeding and sore, and when they are touched, they cause incredible agony. We feel we need to have those wounds bandaged and soothed. We do not want other people touching them – we do not want other people even seeing them. We may feel brittle, and place a protective and defensive wall around ourselves to stop any additional incoming pain. It is actually called 'learning to survive with other people', but it can make us appear curt and short in our response. We may appear distant, off-hand, and sometimes rather rude. Because we can't tell everyone we meet how dreadful we feel (nor would we want to), then they will not understand why we are like this. We can be labelled as 'stand-offish' or 'difficult to get to know'. We feel that the only really safe place is inside ourselves, and so we retreat into our own inner space. We can become very adept at functioning well on a superficial, social level, while actually feeling very little of what is going on around us.

Let us take a look at these feelings of betrayal and rejection, and try to see why they reach so deeply into our psyche, for I think that for many of us the feelings will be remarkably similar, if not the same.

The first thing I want to say about these feelings is that for each person the order of them may vary. Because of our own individuality, we will feel different things at various stages – and not always to the same degree.

For myself, when something awful happens, at first I am very calm. I cope efficiently, remaining outwardly very cool, rather quiet, but seemingly very much in control. Then later, when most other people who have shouted and gone berserk at the beginning, are calming down – I fall apart! Sometimes I wish that in catastrophic situations, I *did* have the ability to get really angry initially, and then cool off. But in these situations, something inside me goes into 'coping mechanisms', and I appear to manage very well.

When I found out about my husband's first affair, I stayed very calm to start with, and immediately tried to 'understand' why he had done this. I tried to work out the best way through for *all* of us. I sat with him, and the 'other woman' and talked about it all. I remember even fetching her some paracetamol because she said she had a headache!

But Brenda, whose story appears in chapter nine, says when she found out about her husband's affair, she felt: 'Very angry with the two people concerned . . . I was also angry at God.'

For myself, after the calmness, I went into delayed shock. Sleep was very difficult. Before my husband had actually left the vicarage, I used to creep into the bathroom and cry as if I would never stop. I was concerned not to wake my girls, or my husband – now I find that pretty amazing! I think I would have been far better if I had kicked him awake too, and said: 'Look what you're doing to me. Help me – you're killing me.'

But it is a peculiar fact about love, that even when we are hurting dreadfully ourselves, we still 'protect' the one we love. I did not want my husband to see the full extent of my pain, in case it hurt or upset *him*! He was the cause of fifty per cent of that pain in the first place!

Would he have acted any differently if I had just sat in front of him and wept uncontrollably? And was there an element of self respect in my not wanting him to see tears? True, I did want to protect him from the effects of his actions, but maybe I also wanted to protect him from the effects those actions were having on me. Maybe I did not want to let him see how much he still mattered to me. After all, by his actions, he was stating loudly and clearly that I did not matter to him. And yet, I told him quite openly that I still loved him every bit as much as I always had. All of which goes to show the underlying, and massive confusion which betrayal brings in its wake. I remember that it all felt like a bad dream, but I was unable to wake up.

I used to walk round the vicarage after he had left, but before I had to dismantle it. I touched every piece of furniture, remembering where and when we had first got it. I thought of those exciting days when we had first moved in, and made it into our home. Every chair, table or bookcase had a story to tell, each one shouted their memories out to me. I truly felt that my heart would burst. It had already been broken, and the sheer agony and pain felt too much to bear. I did not know how I could go on living.

Some of the time I felt numb, and simply could *not* take in the enormity of it all. It was, quite simply, too much, my brain just could not deal with it. This feeling of unreality – of going through the motions of life, but not being involved, is really strange. But what I also found confusing was the way the numbness alternated with a terrible stabbing hurt, which sometimes settled into a deep dragging sadness. I love to paint, and I love colour. If I had to put colours to any of this, the numbness would be grey, the stabbing hurt would be bright red, and the sadness would be a dull brown.

To be honest, the emotions undergo such a battering when we are betrayed by the most loved and important person in our lives, that nothing would ever surprise me about what anyone felt. Christine, whose story appears in chapter ten, used all the following words about her betrayal by her husband: '. . . I felt devastated, betrayed, frustrated, impotent, jealous, angry, resentful and abandoned.'

Rejection robs one of self confidence and self esteem. It gives an inability to do things we would normally take in our stride. We feel unable to go places which we would not usually think twice about. Because the most important person in our lives has stated clearly, by deserting us, that 'I do not want you' then we become afraid to trust other people. They may appear to accept us, but then, so did he/she – when really, they were rejecting us. We ask ourselves, 'Is this person, or this, doing the same?'

We may also feel very stupid. I found myself saying this to my counsellor several times in one session. She asked me why. I was unable to answer. She said that betrayal and rejection do this, because we take on the way our spouses have made us feel by what they have done to us. She has an uncomfortably direct gaze, which on this (as on many other occasions!), she used to very good effect. She held my gaze with her direct look, and said very clearly to me several times: 'You are not stupid.' It felt so good to hear someone I trusted and respected saying that to me. I nearly asked her for it written down, so I could look at it three times a day! A really morale boosting prescription! In fact, as I write, I think maybe I will do that the next time I see her!

I asked myself countless questions – over and over again.

'What have I done? What is it about me he doesn't like, or want? Have I been a bad wife/mother? Is it my fault he's going? If so, what have I done? Why doesn't he love me any more? What have I done wrong? Is it my fault? If so, why? . . .' Over and over it went, on and on, like a refrain. And because I could not come up with the answers, I felt useless, ugly, old, fat, and stupid. All totally false – I do hope so, anyway! I still had all the same talents as before he'd gone – my face; well, he'd always said he thought I was very attractive. Although I never actually agreed with that, I used to love hearing him say it. When my husband left me the first time, I was forty-one, hardly over the hill; I was and still am, dress size twelve – size ten on a good day! And to top all this, I had qualified to join Mensa! But no one could have convinced me that I was not all those negative things I felt.

Our husbands/wives quite literally see every part of

35

us – or very nearly every part. We expose our whole selves in marriage, in a unique way. We are seen by our spouses in many positions of unguarded vulnerability. We have shared our innermost thoughts, given our love in the most powerful way possible, shared our bodies in the most intimate ways, maybe shared part of our spirits too, especially if we have prayed together. All this has been seen by the other – and been rejected. Their opinions of us matter more than anyone else's in the world. Small wonder then, that when they reject all this, we are left feeling worthless, useless, and abandoned. The central core of our being, the very 'essence' of us has been taken – looked at – felt – held – and then smashed to the ground. Rejection feels like being punched in the face, except that it resonates deep within us, and unless we are very fortunate, it affects every part of our minds, emotions, and sometimes, our spirits as well.

There are times when we have to put these feelings of hurt and confusion 'on hold', because in the middle of it all there are decisions – maybe really big ones – to be made.

Both times my husband actually left me (as opposed to the time he promised to come back, and did not) I lost the roof over my head, my job, my church, and my town. There were other things I lost too, but these were the four enormous decisions that I personally had to make, for at a time when all I wanted to do was to crawl into a hole and die, I had to decide in which town to live, and find a house or flat. I had to decide which full time job to go for, when all I wanted to do was sleep – all the time. And I had to find a church where I felt I could worship, and of which I wanted to become a part. There were decisions about separation orders and divorce. There may also be decisions about children to be made, if any young ones are involved.

Then, of course, there is the equally big decision about what to tell people in the new circles in which we find ourselves. If we have children, people will naturally assume we have been married. So they wonder and sometimes you can actually see them doing it, where is her husband? If we have no children, it is equally as difficult to know what to say to people. Join a new church, club, or even street, and people are naturally curious about you – 'the new person'.

I remember the second time my husband left me, I had joined a new church and went away on their parish weekend. It was only a very short while after my husband had left, and I was raw and very careful about what I said, and to whom. I had been talking to a younger woman in the same boat as myself. We had had a really good natter about it all, and had shared with each other some of the horrors of being deserted by our husbands. At that moment, the speaker at the weekend approached us, and as we were all wearing labels, he addressed us by our names. So far, so good! But then he quite suddenly asked us where our husbands were. (I think at that stage, we must have both still have been wearing wedding rings.) My new found friend answered with an amazing speed of thought which I admired tremendously – especially as I was left standing with my mouth opening and shutting like a fish! She looked him full in the face, and said, in a very matter of fact way: 'Actually, they've b . . . . off!' I wanted to applaud! I have to say that later that day – after he had obviously asked the vicar about us, that man showed himself to me as very caring and sensitive, and extremely understanding. I know I learnt that day the motto 'be prepared'. Maybe he learnt something too.

But it did mean being very afraid about what to say, whilst trying to get to know new people. The usual opening remarks are all to do with where we have come from, how long we have lived here, and why we moved. It isn't always appropriate to say 'Actually my husband went off with another woman', and in my case add, 'And I had to move because he was a parish priest, so I had to leave the area' – which wasn't something I particularly enjoyed sharing!

I know there will be others who will identify with my reasons for not wanting to say simply, 'We're separated.' Sometimes, that is true, where there is mutual agreement on both sides. Technically, I left our church owned house a few days before my husband, but his was the desertion – not mine. Desertion of marriage vows, fidelity, and faithfulness. I sometimes did say 'We're separated' but it always went against the grain, for never in a million years would I have ever dreamt of leaving him, or choosing to separate.

Rejection and betrayal are exhausting. We are trying so hard not be betrayed or rejected in every new relationship we make in our new lives as single people, and it is extraordinarily draining and tiring. Trust is not something which is easily come by. It takes time, effort and dedication.

For some, this is simply too much, and they become 'shut-ins', never going out at all – and never risking rejection by others. For those of us who have to support ourselves financially, we have to get out there and get on with it. I don't really know which is worse. I know there certainly were, and still are, days when I simply do not want to face other people. It's just too much effort. Unfortunately, I need my job, so I have to go and I think that to sit at home twiddling my thumbs would be the less healthy option. But oh, how I long some mornings, when the alarm goes off at six, to pull the duvet over my head, and 'switch off' from the world! I know some people reading this will say: 'Well, what is she on about – I'm single/happily married, and I feel like that every morning!' To you I say, 'Join the club!' But I'm not talking about physical weariness, or fatigue – sometimes due to illness. It is more than that. It is feeling unable to face other people. It is not wanting to have to relate to them. Talking feels far too much of an effort, and at these times you do not want people knowing what you think about anything, even the weather! At the heart of it is not wanting to have to express any opinions – either professionally or socially – or make any conversation, because that involves the danger of being rejected again.

It was only much later and slowly at first, when I realised that trusting in new relationships involves risks, and that one must overcome the fear of making mistakes. I learned not to 'hold back' on giving my personality to others and receiving theirs. I may approach all new relationships very cautiously, but this is not always a bad thing, and I feel the friendships I have formed since those early days are the better for it.

Another area of hurt after being married is the way in which some friends, quite unintentionally, reject us. We may have countless dinner parties, cosy suppers, and friends for a meal. It is well known amongst my friends that I have a relentless passion for cooking, and love to entertain and cook for them. I mix couples, sometimes with single friends, sometimes with other couples. Thankfully to date, I haven't had any major personality clashes on my hands – but there is still plenty of time! I love to observe people – they interest me enormously, and part of the fun is planning the guest list. I do get very nervous, and my first foray into entertaining alone left me feeling, hours before my guests had come, that I should have served baked beans on toast! I had chosen what I hoped was a relatively simple, but tasteful menu. In the end it was fine, and I soon got caught up in the creative joy of cooking.

The problem is, that we 'singles' are very rarely asked to dinner parties, supper parties, or what you will. Unless it is by other singles. Full blown parties are fun – they can sometimes be refreshingly anonymous. But we singles have to be asked with someone else, or there is an odd number. I now understand very well why some single people who have never been married, say they are made to feel like second class citizens. And why should we be? Who says this is a world, a society, for couples? The couples themselves of course. We are no less of a person because we are single. In the end, we have to find and make our own social life – more of that in chapter eleven. But being 'left out' hurts, and adds to our own feelings of damaged self-confidence and lack of worth.

Betrayal and rejection bring such a variety of feelings that again, I would not be at all surprised at anything any one said who had experienced them.

Brenda says that when she learnt of her husband's affair she felt: 'Devastated, as though half of myself had been wrenched away, leaving torn flesh.' Brenda's husband was a Church of England lay reader. She says: 'It was unbelievable that a professed man of God could commit such a dreadful sin, not only against me, but against the family of the Church and even against God Himself.'

There once again, is the recurring theme for those of us who are or were church leaders. We feel guilt, because our betrayal resonates out to the church, both locally and on a more global scale as well. There are always, waiting in the wings, those people who are so ready to condemn the church, about anything at all. A vicar or reader who has committed adultery is a gift indeed for them. Hence all the rubbish we read in the tabloid newspapers, whose reporting of clerical indiscretions of any kind seems to have severe problems in keeping away from the realms of fantasy.

Christine, whose husband was neither a vicar or reader says: 'My husband often admitted that he could not cope with marriage (he was a bachelor until quite late on), therefore when he left, I was understanding and supportive. I believed we would retain a committed friendship but live under separate roofs. I would have settled for this 'until death us do part'. It was only later when financial considerations were paramount and solicitors were involved, that my husband and I became estranged. Initially, there was no one else involved, but after two years, my husband moved in with another woman and still lives with her. It was then I felt devastated and betrayed . . .'

The experience of each of us affects us in many different ways, depending on our circumstances and our personalities. Through it there are recurring themes – similarities which we all may feel to differing degrees. But there are no rules, and any feeling we experience is valid, because it is our own personal reaction to what has happened to us as a unique person. No one has the right to say to us: 'You should not feel like that as a Christian . . .' or indeed: 'If you really are a Christian you must feel this, or this . . .' We are all individuals, and we are as God has made us. We feel what we feel. It is what we do with those feelings that is important.

Robert, who tells his story in chapter twelve, is a clergyman whose wife left him for another man. He said that when he realised that his wife was becoming attracted to another man he felt '. . . sad, and something of a failure . . . I felt guilty that my lifestyle as a clergyman was mainly to blame for things . . . but even now, I don't believe I could have stopped it. It was her escape route and she was determined to take it.'

Confusion, guilt, grief, frustration, fear, severe emotional pain – the list is endless. But for all of us there is a feeling of shock, of disbelief, or unreality. A feeling that 'This cannot be happening to me'. Then immediately, or later on, come the feelings of worthlessness, uselessness, and loss of self confidence.

I sometimes think how amazing it is that something we find out in one day can change our whole lives, including our perception of ourselves. It may well have been going on for years, but for all of us there is that certain moment in time when we finally know. And in that moment is born the beginning of frighteningly deep feelings and pain about ourselves. Obviously I cannot speak for other people. All I can say for myself is that it will take many years for the scars to heal – and it may not be until I meet my God face to face. There are still many times when I feel the effects of being betrayed and rejected. I still 'take offence' far too easily. I feel 'left out' of things very quickly, and then feel extremely stupid when it becomes obvious there was a valid reason for it. I know others will be able to identify with my feelings of lack of self confidence, over sensitivity to criticism, and sometimes, even now, pure shame. Not shame for myself, but for the effect of what has happened on so many other people. And for the shame it has brought on the Church of God, and sometimes, I think, on the very name of God Himself.

Maybe, just maybe, it will help someone to know this. You are not alone. What you are experiencing is normal, and those of us who feel, or have felt the same, reach out to you.

And you are not alone on another level. Whatever you think about God at these times, the simple fact is: HE IS THERE WITH, AND FOR YOU. If you remember nothing else, remember this. When He hung on the Cross, He faced the ultimate betrayal and rejection, by His friends, by His race, and worst of all, by His heavenly Father. God is part of Christ, and Christ is part of God – and there was this terrible separation. Separated from part of Himself – rejected by part of Himself. There can be no greater betrayal than this, and we can never experience anything a fraction as devastating. So not only has Christ suffered in all ways as we do, but He has suffered a hundred thousand times more He has been all the way – and beyond, for us – for you. Maybe we feel too bad to pray, or go to church. Maybe the very last thing we want to do is to mix with a load of other Christians! Don't worry, that's O.K. But if we can just hold on to the fact that He is there, then He will hold on to us and never let us go.

The poem which ends this chapter may seem like a

contradiction of what I have just said, but that is not so – because of the last line. The resurrection spoken of in this poem is our own personal one as well as the final one. It does not mean that we stay dead, numb, and empty. In His time God will bring about our resurrection – He will raise us up. But because He is God, He will know when we are healed enough to do this. And He, above all others, knows just how long that healing will take. For me, I am content to wait.

Betrayal

Pushed aside
Like a used rag or
A dirty shirt.
No longer wanted
Thought of or
Loved.

Feelings not considered
Not important
Any more.
I don't matter now.
Treated, dealt with
Anyhow.

Like a spider
Squashed and trodden underfoot
No consideration given
To the pain –
Because from now on he doesn't
Care.

Selfishness means
He closes his eyes to
My feelings.
Where once I was important
Now I cease to
Exist.

Feel like nothing
Don't want to live
I must be worthless
He's walking away.
Do I exist – I don't think so.
Rejection.

Left for dead.
Might as well be.
Where once I was loved
Now I clutter his life.
No pain worse than
Betrayal.

Numbness.
Emptiness.
Just nothing.
Nothing
Nothing
Betrayal
And death.

I wait for the resurrection.

Chapter Three

EXPECTATIONS AND RESPONSE

I sat in the vicarage lounge. It was six a.m. on a cold December morning. The early prayer meeting had just begun and people were suggesting topics for prayer. There was a pause, and suddenly someone said: 'I think we should pray for Christian marriages. I've heard Satanists in this area are praying for their breakup.'

The pain shot through me like a knife. I wanted to scream: 'But that's what happened to me. *We* were told Satanists in our area were praying for the breakdown of clergy marriages.' I do not know if the person concerned knew what had happened to me, but I wanted to say: 'Please don't ignore me. I still hurt. I want to pray for Christian marriages more than anyone, but please don't ignore the fact that you have someone in the group who has experienced this. Pray for me too. Name it, name me, for because of it my life will never be the same again.'

I am very aware that we who have been deserted by our spouses, we who are divorced, are an embarrassment to other people who simply do not know how to treat us, or relate to us. I learnt very early on, that often, we have to tell people how we want to be treated. They may skirt round it – not meet our eyes – look awkward. It is like crossing the road when we see someone coming who has recently been bereaved. If only others realised that a hug speaks far more eloquently than a thousand words!

The other thing which is not always appreciated is

the length of time the pain goes on at a very intense level. The incident above took place some three and a half years after my husband left me. Because of the completeness of the trauma, because it does alter our whole lives, it is difficult for others to understand. Many problems involve only one area of our lives, but marriage breakdown is our whole lives. I remember when it happened to me the first time, my husband said: 'You'll have massive support from the parish. They'll all be on your side.' Naïvely I believed him. How wrong I was. Sometimes we are in for very pleasant surprises, but also some very nasty shocks indeed.

It is a strange, but true fact, that we do not find out who our real friends are until the chips are down and life is stacked up against us. Some of the people I thought would support me most caused me the greatest distress, whilst people I had previously only called acquaintances turned out to be really understanding and supportive, and have since become good friends.

It all hinges on the fact that in marriage breakdown, as with all major traumas, no one else can really appreciate the depth of pain unless they've experienced it first hand. It is totally impossible for others to realise how much like a drowning person we feel. I know others to whom the same thing has happened, and they withdrew and kept themselves from any one-to-one contact. For those who know of the Myers-Briggs personality typing, I am an 'I', which stands for Introverted, as opposed to 'E' which stands for Extroverted. These words are not used in the usual way. It means in Myers-Briggs terminology, that extroverts gain inner strength and are resourced by being with others, and introverts gain their energy from being alone. But even being an 'I', never in my life have I needed other people so much as the three times my husband left me. It may sound really awful now, but even though there were some people I instinctively kept away from, there were others to whom I almost clung – just to stay alive. It would have been so *very* easy to just sit down and give up. True, I did think about the effect on my family and close friends of what was happening to me, for their grief hurt me too, and I wanted to spare them that. But the problem is so 'global', that in the sea of uncertainties in which I found myself, I would have clung to anything which would have helped me stay afloat. Maybe people in my position do 'use' friends at a time like this, but I remember I hoped that all my friends would understand the *huge* effort in just staying alive. Unfortunately for me, this was not so.

I really thought that as the 'innocent party', as the deserted wife of their vicar, friends in the parish would support and help me. Ultimately, they did and they were lovely and caring, but something happened in between, which to this day I still cannot fully believe, and which meant that the support I so desperately needed was delayed in manifesting itself. The church in which we were serving at the time was an evangelical one, and I had heard an awful lot debated, preached, and said about love – and that is what I expected to receive as soon as my husband left the vicarage.

We had all gone away for a fortnight to escape from the intrusiveness of the media. On our return my husband left the vicarage, and I was left alone with my two daughters.

Before we had gone away, a little group of 'friends' had promised on my return to be my support group. We had met weekly during all my years in the parish to pray together. There were promises of help in finding a new home and decorating it. Promises of help with the girls. Promises of help finding a job. Promises of help with everything. They told me I would not need other people, they would be my helpers and support. After my husband left that night, I immediately went up to see my girls who were in their bedroom together.

There were some tears I remember, and some talking. I then rang one of these 'friends' who had promised so much. Imagine my horror on being told, no, she could not come round – she was busy. In the days and weeks that followed, that little group of people did a complete 'U' turn. If my husband, by his behaviour, had taken me to the gates of hell, they, by their behaviour, pushed me in.

I was told by them that I had to be 'swept aside' in order for the parish to heal. One of them even called at the vicarage, stood at the front door, and told me I was 'tainted with my husband's sin'. I was told 'there can be no healing all the time people can see you', and many other similar little gems!

Despite the fact that I could not change my girls' school because my elder daughter was studying for her G.C.S.E.s, one of them wrote to me begging me 'not to let Satan divide us'. The letter said we could not remain friends(!) unless I did what *they* said and moved out of the parish. I felt like so much dross to be swept aside. I later discovered that they had told several key people in the church not to speak to me or visit me because I had to be 'swept aside'. It seemed they would not listen to the Bishop or anyone else.

If any one of them had even the slightest clue as to how I felt because of my husband's desertion and rejection, all they would have done would have been to hold me while I wept. But the only time one of them *did* see me cry, she said she could not bear it, and I was left distraught and uncomforted. If any one of them had even the tiniest inkling of the enormous pain and added rejection they caused me, they would have been banging on my door and begging for forgiveness, not banging on it to tell me I was 'tainted with my husband's sin'.

I think this is a very extreme example of what can happen and I would hate anyone not to trust their friends when they need them the most. We have to, and I was just extraordinarily unfortunate that this happened to me. It did not help my ability to trust people again, and almost drove me insane with grief. I do so wish they could have understood how their behaviour nearly destroyed me, for I missed their friendship and would have given anything for it not to have ended that way. One thing it *did* do was to make me feel with *real* empathy with Our Lord's intense loneliness in the Garden of Gethsemane. Then His friends slept while He needed their support, and deserted Him when He needed their love the most, leaving Him to be crucified alone.

To counter this very negative response, I must go on to say that my family and nearly all of my friends simply could not do enough for me.

You will find that when the news first leaks out that you are 'on your own' whether it is a mutual decision or you have been deserted, the response you will get will be very mixed. Women especially are very keen to want the woman to take the blame. I think this is because in some way I do not fully understand, if the woman is to blame this helps them to feel more secure. If they admit that the man is to blame, then this means that there is the possibility that *their* husbands could be at fault within their own marriages. But if it is the woman's fault, consequently in their minds, it could never happen to them, because they tell themselves *they* would never do anything to cause their husbands to leave. If they convince themselves of this, then it means that their marriage is under their control. This is one explanation behind women wanting to blame the wife in marriage breakdown. I think their premise is a false one, but it would be a brave married woman who would admit it!

I was visiting a close friend, and we were talking about other people's response to the news of my husband's leaving for the second time, and going off with another woman. There was what is always called in books 'a pregnant pause'. Then quietly and very matter of factly, my friend told me what another woman friend had said on hearing the news. And this person had experienced the trauma of divorce for themselves. It went something on the lines of: 'Well, it can't have all been his fault. It never is. She must be to blame too. There'll be a reason why he went.' There was. It was approximately five feet six tall, and *very* determined to get him! I was very hurt at the time by this comment, but I think it is a good example of another woman wanting me to be to blame.

One of the areas of difficulty in marriage breakdown is that of joint friends. Of course, it depends very much on the circumstances. For myself, among the tremendous number of friends we had made in the five parishes in which we served, plus all the other friends we had, I can only think of two couples who have taken my husband's side, as it were. The facts have spoken for themselves, and only two people have actually had the effrontery to tell me to my face that they thought I was wrong to take my husband back after two years. My reply to them both was exactly the same then as it would be today. It is absolutely nothing to do with anyone else except my husband and I. One relationship above all which is sacrosanct, in terms of decisions taken, is marriage. We can listen to advice, we can pray, we may read books, but some things are decisions of the heart, and are uniquely individual. We never have to explain to anyone the reasons for anything we do, if we do not wish to. I did not explain it then, and I doubt if I would now, if challenged again. All I know is, my love would not allow me to say 'no'. I believe in marriage with all my heart. I also believe in forgiveness. Perhaps equally as important as these, I could not have lived with myself if I had not given my husband a second chance. Everyone deserves that.

The difficulty for us as Christians is that Christ said: 'forgive seven times seventy.' I am well known for my problems with figures, but that makes, I believe, four hundred and ninety! But here we must exercise discretion. There are many examples of marital breakdown in which it would be pure idiocy to keep forgiving. To watch our spouses go out and repeatedly commit adultery, then say: 'I've only forgiven you three hundred and ten times, one hundred and eighty to go!' is patently ridiculous. Christ has very definite things to say about adultery, the main one being to the woman caught in the act: 'Go your way . . . AND SIN NO MORE.' For true forgiveness, there has to be true repentance. Not always a popular word. Repentance is the honest intention not to commit the act again, not every intention of doing it again regularly. Anyone who repeatedly commits adultery whether it is many times with the same woman, or once with many different women, is making a nonsense of what our Lord tells us to do.

Of *course* there is never a completely 'innocent party'. We are all guilty of all kinds of things, and marriage is no exception to this. But there is an innocent party if one is staying true to the marriage vows and faithful to the spouse. My husband and I were happy together. After he came back, one friend said she had never seen him so happy, and had never seen him laugh so much. For starters, we were always very good friends – we laughed a lot together, and had fun. Many marriages fail for the lack of friendship and fun. We had our explosive moments, but we did not have endless rows – our marriage did not falter, crumble and die. It died because two people killed it – and I was not one of them. But in marriage, even if there are rows – even if one party is difficult to live with – even if they are massively untidy – always leave the top off the toothpaste – grab all the duvet every night – snore – make a noise when they eat – fly off the handle easily – put the other person down – have a hundred and one irritating habits – NOTHING is sufficient reason for a person to commit adultery.

Other people's responses can be terribly hurtful. True, we all speak and react because we are carrying our own 'baggage', but like the Bishop said: 'Love is seeing with the eyes of those it loves.' Not seeing with our own eyes, then visiting that vision on to someone else. An American called David Biebel has written a superb book on suffering called *If God Is So Good, Why Do I Hurt So Bad?*[2], in which he tells of the death of one son from a genetic illness, and the suffering of a second son from the same disease. In it he says that 'the church is the only club which shoots its wounded in the back.' I think we need to remember that, when we hear of one of its members suffering a misfortune.

Brenda, whose husband, although not a vicar, was in a position of leadership in the church, had a very different experience to mine when her husband left her for another woman. She found that everyone in the church was very supportive and understanding. They all stood by her, and she felt loved and supported. As with all major traumas, one thing that does happen is that it can make us far more understanding of others to whom the same thing has happened. We really can enter into their pain – and they in turn can feel this empathy. I remember recently when my elder daughter's heart was broken by a man she loved very much. Any mother would feel for her child, but she knew that I understood her pain so intimately, because I had been there myself. We don't necessarily need words to express our empathy – arms come into their own at these times. I wrote a poem when it happened to my daughter, and she has given me permission to use it here.

My Daughter

Her eyes were full of pain, my daughter –
She searched my face for signs of hope
– for an answer

She asked me why he was acting this way
I said 'People change'
Again she asked me why
– and I had no answer.

She asked if it would ever stop
hurting.
I told her one day she
would want to live again.
She said she was exhausted
and asked when it would stop
– I had no answer
except perhaps: 'One day, one day.'

She said she could not understand it,
I said I could not
either.

Over and over we went
and then she wept –
and I held her close
– and she clung to me
we wept together
and we clung together
until my arms ached
– and then I went on holding
– just like You Father, just like You

Then I told her the only answer
I have
– I told her I will always be there
for her –
And as I held her, I told her
I loved her
– I said it over and over again
'I love you, I love you, I love you'
until it was all that she could hear –
Just like You Father
Just like You

53

We need to surround ourselves, yes, with God's love of course, but also with the human 'evidence' of that love, as shown through other people. It is difficult knowing who will help us in the best way – especially at a time when because of what has happened we are finding it incredibly hard to trust other people at all. I had a little group who stood by me through thick and thin – through good times and bad. We didn't always agree on everything, but we respected each other's differences – which is, after all, a sign of a healthy friendship. I knew I could trust these people because of their unconditional love and acceptance in the past. People like my Christian doctor and his wife, who always welcome me with open arms, and make me feel special. They and other friends phone every so often just to see if I'm all right, and if I'm not they let me tell it how it is. As time has gone on, I have made new friendships and in the five years since my husband left, there are now other people in my life who help me as well. Often it is a mutual support – each helping the other through bad times.

One of these new friends introduced me to my counsellor, Cath, a wonderful down to earth, but incredibly sensitive Christian, whose faith brooks no nonsense, and whose knowledge of God is very intimate. Without her wisdom and support, I don't think I would have stayed sane – if, indeed, I have! I owe her a huge debt of gratitude, as I do my vicar and his wife whose door is always open if I need them, and whose love and acceptance has soothed my hurts on many occasions – and Linda, our lady curate, now a close friend of mine, who is always only a phone call away. With these and other friends moments of tears and laughter are shared together, and I am more thankful than I can ever say to them all.

Several very good friends said I could ring them at any time of the day or night. And I knew I could. I knew I could 'phone, or go round, or they came to see me, and this is still so today. I know we are all different in this respect, but I needed help – and I knew it. I did not have people round me all the time, because I also needed a lot of space. I seem to remember I spent a lot of time simply gazing into space. Just breathing – just living. Anything else was too painful.

It was also very important for me to have those around me who respected my pain and weren't too keen to tell me to 'pull myself together' or 'look on the bright side', or other such meaningless phrases, or who said a quick prayer and expected it to be all right. We are almost indescribably vulnerable at a time like this, and it would be emotional suicide to share our hurt with those who do not understand it or try to belittle it. Cliff and Sylvia were superb in this respect, because they used to just hold me. I think often Sylvia's arms must have ached after I left their house. But that was exactly what I needed. Someone to help 'contain' me, and the dreadful agony I felt inside. I didn't really need people to help me to laugh. Apart from being false anyway, it was not necessary, because I did laugh often, and with different people. There is a sort of 'black' humour which surfaces when the odds are stacked against you. Anyway why not laugh? What else had I to lose?

As time went on, my support group changed – well, some of them, and some remained the same. This was important too, because whilst I wanted some who had been with me as my life changed, I needed new friends to help me with new situations. It's quite hard for some of us to learn to reach out and say 'Please help me', but it brings great rewards of unexpected kinds to 'asker' and giver alike. So I consider it really important to select a group of trusted friends – but do make sure they are the right ones. The fact is we learn intuitively who we can trust and with whom we feel safe. I think the general rule is, if you are in any doubt about sharing yourself with someone at a deeper level than everyday conversation – don't. Don't be afraid to trust, but be cautious. It is a bit of a tightrope, but generally it's those folk who *do* phone when they say they will, who *do* invite you out, who *do* make you feel both wanted and accepted, who *do* make you feel they have time for you – not the ones who only talk about it. People with whom you feel 'safe' – both when you're with them, and with the knowledge of what you have shared with them after they have gone. I will never be able to thank all my friends enough for all the love and support they have given and are still giving me. There may well be those of you who feel totally alone or isolated. I would urge you to reach out to someone, or a group to help you. The local vicar, priest or minister, or your own GP is often a good place to start. At the back of this book there is a list of 'Help Agencies', groups who can be contacted for various reasons. When we are completely alone, we need at least to feel there is someone we can phone – some other person to help us at the 'other end of the line'. The Citizens' Advice Bureaux also have large amounts of information about such things as counsellors if you need one, or various help groups. Do reach out and find the help you deserve if you are isolated for whatever reason.

I have written a lot about words and what we say to each other. I would like to end this chapter with a poem about just one word. Maybe at the end of the day it is the word all the others must point to. It is the only word of which we can have 'great expectations' and never be disappointed in the response.

One Word

It is just a word –
A rather small word really –
And yet the biggest word from the beginning of time
The most precious word that will ever be in all
eternity.

Within it is contained the suffering of the world.
For every problem, every question, each unspoken
cry
– It is the answer.
Each anguished scream torn from a mind in pain,
Each broken cry which comes from a bleeding
heart,
Each shout of anger at injustices felt,
Each bewildered question at the events of life,
All, and all, are met in that one single word.

It holds, that word, every joy that has ever been,
And all the happiness of life sings in a song
of praise.
Each newborn baby's cry is heard with wonder,
Each innocent child's act of love is held within it,
And laughter and peace join hands and dance
together
In a love song of wonder and praise of the word.

Its power can heal the deepest hurt,
Its gentleness can soothe the troubled mind.
Just to speak the word can push the darkness back,
To hear it whispered brings light into the pain.
It gives meaning to all unanswered questions,
And reason to things that cannot be explained.

It is just a word –
A rather small word really.
But it is everything –
The beginning and the end which never ends
– One death – one life – one Lord –
One word –
JESUS.

Chapter Four

FEELINGS CHRISTIANS 'SHOULDN'T' HAVE (I)

GUILT – THE CHRISTIAN DILEMMA

I do not know why it is, but many of us who follow the
Christian faith have a large overdose of guilt.
Whenever anything happens we leap in, saying 'Oh
sorry, it's my fault . . . !' I even found myself apologising to a lady in Sainsburys, because she had pushed *her*
trolley into *my* ankle! I stood there reeling with pain,
feeling at the very least she had fractured it and thinking 'Why don't people look where they're going?!' Yet
I heard myself saying, as I leant on my trolley for support, 'Oh, sorry . . . !' We seem to want to take the
blame for everything from the beginning of creation.
And I think that therein lies a clue.

Those who have been brought up in the more
evangelical wing of the Church of England, or the non-
conformist churches, have heard literally hundreds of
sermons on sin. They have heard how Eve first
committed it, and how she enticed Adam to do the
same. They have heard how certain thoughts and feelings can be sins. They have listened to hours of being
told to repent, and even more hours of being told they
have 'to change'. Small wonder many have deep com-
plexes about how they are not all right and acceptable
as people. Obviously we have to let God have His way
in our lives, and be open to any changes He may want

to make, but it is so easy to get the idea that we have to change in every way. Some people even get to feel that God cannot love them as they are, when in fact the opposite is true, and He loves us exactly where and who we are.

It is often bellowed from the pulpit that if we want or 'desire' something, then it must be wrong. We feel as if God always wants us to choose the most difficult path, and if anything at all goes wrong in our lives, we are more than ready to blame ourselves.

Those of the 'higher' church persuasion can find themselves in just as much trouble. Making one's confession through a priest entails a very detailed look at the way we live. A close examination to see where we have 'erred and strayed from Thy ways', can all too easily become beating ourselves – metaphorically speaking – across the back over supposed sins, just as much as the early mystics did with their very real flagellums! Or like wearing hair shirts as a sign of repentance! Formal confession is of inestimable value, but there are times when we feel the list of sins is rather short, and we can start making ourselves feel guilty over imagined or imaginary wrongs, so as to present a more 'worthy' list!

We tie ourselves in knots because as Christians we feel we 'shouldn't' feel certain things. The truth is that we do not have some heavenly immunity from human emotions. Christ suffered, and was tested, in all ways as we are. It is what we *do* with the emotions that matters.

It is my privilege to listen and share with those who are, or have, experienced marriage breakdown. How often have I heard someone say, as I have sat listening, 'I know I *shouldn't* feel like that but . . .' We think, and feel, and are troubled, by all the same emotions as every other human being on the planet. There is not one set of emotions for non-Christians, and a different one for Christians! We are exempt from nothing. God would not have gone to all the trouble of sending Jesus as a human if He wanted us to bypass our humanity. The difference for us is how Christ tells us to deal with these things.

There is such a lot of 'false guilt' about. We Christians are also really very good at imposing it on others. Sometimes we are made to feel guilty because we are in pain and we are honest about it. More than once, at a prayer meeting, Christian talk, or teaching evening, someone will say something like: 'Oh, Vera is *so* wonderful! My word, how she's suffered, but you never hear her complain. She's always so radiant!' I absolutely hate remarks like that! I would have strong feelings of dislike for the 'Vera's' of this world, except I think the really radiant ones – the real 'Vera's' – would hate to be spoken of in this way in the first place!

We *do* need to hear of those whose faith is really helping them, but not, as so often seems to happen, in an accusatory type of way. There are many of us whose faith is the only thing that has kept us going. The one thing we *can* do with our pain is to be honest about it. By this, I do not mean sharing it with everyone we meet. How boring we would be! And we would very soon wonder why we were so often alone if we did – and deservedly so! We all know those folk to whom it is definitely a mistake to say 'How are you?'!

By speaking the truth about our pain, we often become a threat to others. Some people can only deal with their own pain if they keep the lid on – tight. Sooner or later, of course, there will be an explosion of one kind or another. Pain, like yeast, ferments. It either causes us to rise and grow, and become well proved bread, or it gets too hot, or cold, and dies. The bread has no air, no lift, no lightness. Know folk like that? I do.

David Biebel writes[3]: 'All around us, people are in pain. Emotional, physical, relational, spiritual – whatever its source, the pain feels the same.'

Even born-again, sincere, evangelical, Bible-believing, church-going, church-leading believers are in pain. 'There's a broken heart in every pew' said Joseph Parker, a nineteenth-century British pastor. And it's still true today.

Unfortunately, as Biebel also noted, 'The church is the only club that shoots its wounded in the back, and the unrealistic expectations or even rejection that sometimes masquerade as spirituality can bring further injury instead of healing to people who desperately need it.'

There are appropriate and inappropriate places to show or express our hurt. No good walking round Sainsburys, list in one hand, hanky in the other, crying as we choose breakfast cereals and soap powders alike! How embarrassing for other shoppers! Much better to hurry the shopping, even if we do forget the coffee, stay 'dry', then go round to a trusted friend and cry our hearts out!

It is strange, is it not, that we for whom the most precious moment on earth is sharing together in receiving the broken body of Christ, should then continue to be together, and hide our own brokenness from each other. The priest says, at the heart of the Eucharist, 'The body of Christ . . . BROKEN FOR YOU.' It is the very essence of our Christian faith. Together we sing that lovely chorus about breaking the bread, drinking the cup, and sharing together in the body of Christ. Then we go and have a coffee after the service, 'shut down', and hide our brokenness from the very people with whom we have just shared the broken body of Christ. Isn't it bizarre?

David Biebel writes[4]: 'If pain is a place where we meet each other in humanity and even meet with God, why does speaking the truth about it sometimes sound like heresy, blasphemy, or worse? And why are hurting people sometimes asked, expected, or required to pretend about the way they really feel, when telling the truth is closer to Godliness than pretending will ever be.'

Whether it was illness, death, separation, divorce, infidelity, treachery, financial ruin, betrayal, or any other loss that brought your pain, somebody probably tried to 'comfort' you with words like these: 'All things work together for good'. Or 'keep your eyes on Jesus and everything will be all right.' And you nodded. What else could you do? They were telling the truth, after all.

But did they really want *you* to tell the truth – that is, if you could even put it into words?

It's doubtful.

Very few people are willing to listen, to truly hear your lament, to feel your anguish and share the pain, to cry with you until *you* have decided it's time to stop.

What happens for most hurting believers as a result is that they end up embracing only half the paradox of pain:

– Sometimes life is agony.

– Our loving God is in control.'

How amazingly true this is. Often we are made to feel guilty by the very people who should be staying with us the most. IT IS POSSIBLE FOR LIFE TO HURT, AND GO ON HURTING, AND FOR GOD TO STILL BE IN CONTROL. Maybe that statement, more than any other, is the one I would like to make my leitmotiv. From where did we get our almost immutable idea that the Christian life is pain free? I think every Bible should have a 'Government Health Warning' on it! 'Reading this can seriously affect your life. Pain content: Very high. God content: Higher'!!

Why is it so hard for some of us to grasp that life can hurt and go on hurting, and for that not to be a denial of God's presence, but an affirmation of it?

Brenda speaks very movingly of her feelings of guilt when her husband left her. She says: 'I felt guilty for being angry; not being able to cope – as a Christian we think the "world" expects us to cope. The continual weeping, swift changes of mood, guilt at feeling "cut off from God", not able to pray. Guilt for not being able to rely completely on God.'

I was devastated once when someone prayed for me at a prayer meeting, 'I pray, Lord, that Sue will have peace, deep peace. I pray for her Lord, for sometimes the peace is not always there.' My overriding feeling was not that of 'deep peace', but of more pain and sheer frustration! I had an almost irresistible urge to shout very loudly, 'You try my .... life!'

The Christian life is not primarily about peace. It is about love. It takes a very mature and sacrificial love to accept another Christian's lack of abiding peace about life's sometimes excruciating circumstances, AND NOT TO MAKE THEM FEEL GUILTY. My heart can be – it isn't always – but it *can* be, at deep peace with God about my relationship with Him. I may know that *nothing* can separate me from the love of God, and I can feel Him right within me; and I can still be in deep, deep pain.

Does it make it wrong, because in the depths of pain which abandonment brings, we who have travelled those places have been shown hidden truths? Are the treasures of darkness we find so unpalatable? Christ, as God, knew He had not come to bring peace and ease for His children. Christ, as man, experienced for Himself the deep and lasting pain of rejection, desertion and abandonment. 'Could you not watch with me one short hour?' (Mark 14 v 37). I cry out on behalf of all those who hurt, and go on hurting, 'Watch with us – stay with our pain, our sometimes lack of peace. Accept how we say it is, and do not demean us or accuse us of lack of faith. Help us unwrap the jewels of the deep dark places, for they shine more brightly for having been so long in the dark.'

And to those still in that place, to those who are only just hanging on, I say IT'S ALL RIGHT. People may not understand, but God does. He's hanging in there with you. I would give you 'permission' to go on hurting, but I don't have to. He already has. 'Come to me, all of you who are tired from carrying heavy loads, and I will give you rest'. (Matthew 11 v 28). Notice not 'I will take your burden away', but '. . . give you rest . . .' – to help you carry it. If Christ does not wave a heavenly wand and make it all right, then why do we think we can? Or worse still, that it doesn't matter? Tell them to trust God and they'll be O.K. Wrong. Stay with them where they are, and you will have shown Christ's love so clearly, He'll lead you both on a little way. Much better!

I wrote the following poem when I was suffering from an 'overdose' of other people! I was utterly worn out, and very fed up with people implying I had not got enough faith because I could not smile and say: 'Life is wonderful. I'm in the pits, and I'm so happy about it!' I think it expresses what I'm struggling to say here.

Keep Me Weak, Lord

Lord, it's bad – very bad.

It takes so much time and energy to hold my arms
out to Your cross.
I feel almost too tired even to look at You –
But as I do I see that Your head is bowed too
under the weight of the burden You are carrying.

I can only come to the foot of Your cross in weakness –
I can only be there at Your feet my Saviour
underneath Your broken body
in my own brokenness, anguish, and despair.
And then, my Saviour, my pain rises up to meet Yours
– and Yours comes down to embrace me
and I know in that moment, in a blinding flash,

that You understand completely –
that Your compassion embraces all my needs.

I don't have to tell You that in my total weakness
and grief
You are the only One who can take my fullest honesty –
I don't have to tell You that if I let go and stop
struggling
– if I 'give in', it doesn't mean I can't feel You.
I don't have to tell You that in that moment of total
abandonment to You –
You are nearer to me than ever before.

You understand my struggles to be honest
– to myself – to others – and to You.
You understand that being honest about my feelings
is the way to see You more clearly,
it isn't a denial of Your presence –
it's an affirmation of it –
and it hurts when others don't understand this.
They seem to think that by being honest I'm not
depending on You.
They start telling me to 'Take it to the Lord',
or to 'Lean on God'.
How can I take it to You when You allowed it all,
in the first place?

I hurt – I ache in every part, but this is the way to You.
Each new heartache, each tearing memory, draws
me closer to You.
I know my pain shows on my face –
but I know You showed Your pain when You were
on the cross.
The serene patient look takes longer to achieve
than the honest wearing of myself on my face.

I know Father that You are there changing me –
I'm sure the wonderful serene bit takes so much longer –

> *but that's all right – that's all right –*
> *for I know You aren't worried about that.*
> *All You need is for me to be willing.*
> *So keep me weak Lord – keep me weak –*
> *For it's only in that weakness that I'm strong enough*
> *to be broken*
> *– and it's only in that brokenness that truly and*
> *completely*
> *I am Yours – I am Yours – I am Yours.*

I would not like to be misunderstood here. In the absence of Christ in human form, other people are what keep many of us going. True, we can get down on our knees and pray, but there are those times when we all need the 'solidarity' of another person.

Friends and other people (provided they are the right ones!), are very necessary to us if we are having a bad day – especially if the bad day is because we are having a 'guilt trip'. There are still some days, even five years on, especially if I am very tired, when the whole thing seems just too much. Maybe I've heard a tune on the radio, maybe a certain smell has drifted in through the window, maybe for no particular reason – except the little matter of twenty-five years together, my husband will suddenly intrude into my thoughts. Then the mind goes crazy, and I start remembering. I can say to myself – sometimes I do it aloud for extra impact: 'Sue, get a grip. Remembering like this is the fast road to trouble. Turn it off, look forward, and get on with your life.' The trouble is that there is also someone else in my head who starts saying; 'Well, if it had not been for what has happened, for the actions of two other people, you would not be here in this place at this time. You would not be getting up at a ridiculously early hour each day, driving fifteen miles to work, then doing a full time job. In fact,' the voice goes on, 'nothing in your life would be as it is now. You would not be in this place, this town. No day, or night, for that matter, will ever be the same again because of what has happened.'

Some people may say: 'Well, that's self-pity if ever I heard it.' It isn't. Self-pity is wallowing, and hating every moment of your 'now'. I do not hate each moment. Much of it I enjoy very much. When I am teaching sacred dance, or when I am dancing myself, I am extremely happy. In fact, I am never so full of real joy, or feel as close to God, as when I am dancing in worship. Just to move to a song about Him, for me, seems to bring heaven down, and earth reaches up to join with it, and I am caught up in some place with Him. I feel I could touch Him with my slightest breath, because He is so near, so 'within', and I do not feel as though I am here at all, but somewhere very 'other'. More than anything else in the whole world I love to dance – it is when I feel most alive. So at those times I can actually thank God, not for what has happened of course, but for where I am and the time I am in now.

There are several new areas of ministry that I do not think I would be able to be developing if life had stayed the same for me. Not that I am trying to give anyone an escape route, it is simply that God uses everything in our lives. There are no waste bins in heaven! God uses anything and everything. He takes the shattered remains of our lives and does something wonderful with them. We may not realise it at the time, because we are still hurting. Sometimes he takes the pieces and uses them still in their shattered form, and our lives become a sacrifice for Him, broken, not whole. But it is that very brokenness which is our greatest gift to God, and the thing He wants the most.

It is a very short bus ride from tiredness to guilt. It is, I am sure, also a very devious route, because for the life of me, I cannot quite follow it, even though I have a season ticket on that particular bus! I *think* it is linked to those two old sign posts, betrayal and rejection, and I *think* it goes something like this.

When everything we are has been taken, examined,

lived with, and accepted, and then that acceptance changes, something in us changes too. The person we love most in the whole world has changed their perception of us. Quite why, I think only the psychologists could tell us. It may be something to do with someone else waiting in the wings, which must be flattering for them, and alters how they think about things. Sometimes it just happens. They change. Very hastily. I add here that this is not a reason for 'changing partners'. Nothing is sufficient reason for that. I think the only exception to this statement are those instances of violence, and cruelty of any kind. Also any problems with alcohol, or if one partner changes their sexual orientation. Then it is a different thing altogether. There are instances when it would be both unsafe and unwise to stay with our spouses, and I for one do not advocate staying together at any price.

When thinking about divorce, in Matthew's famous exception phrase (Matthew 5 v 32), he states: 'If a man (woman) divorces his (her) wife (husband) for any cause other than his (her) unfaithfulness . . .' Many Christians not only desert their spouses, but they do not bother to wait until they are divorced before moving in with their new partner.

So I think when our spouse's opinion of us changes, and we cannot understand why this is, and because we are hurting so much, we have to have *something* to blame. There isn't anything else, so we start to blame ourselves. We say: 'If he/she has changed in his/her feelings towards me, it has to be my fault.' It isn't really a reason, but at the time it feels like it. We cannot bear to think that something is radically wrong with them because we love them. And love is awfully good at making excuses for the one it loves. Sometimes we look at a couple and wonder what on earth they see in each other! It is indeed true that when we first fall in love, love can indeed be blind. It is only later on that the trouble starts, and after waking up morning after morning to the things we were blind to at first, and that have suddenly become all too obvious, we realise that he/she is not Mr or Mrs Perfect after all! It's then that marriage really begins. It's the learning to love, both in spite of, and because of, those bits we do not like. I think for some, this is just too difficult, and they give up and look elsewhere for someone else. But that does not mean that we are any less of a person because they decide they will not work on any areas of difficulty. A good talk over a drink with our spouses could often save so much heartache. Telling each other in honesty, what it is in the other that we feel we cannot stand any longer, can be very painful, but it can also be very con-structive. It is not a slanging match – we can also tell each other their good points, but an honest attempt to improve our marriage. And let's face it, they *all* need that, don't they? I always get very worried and suspi-cious when I hear someone say, 'Oh, we never row. We've been married for sixty years, and we've never had a cross word!' I find myself wondering just what that relationship is really like. Some may say, 'Well, she's a fine one to talk, her husband walked out on her.'

But that last comment is exactly what we are talking about here. Taking on false guilt. The fact that our spouses have left us for their own reasons – be it a 'who' or a 'what', does not make us any the less of a person.

It would be oh, so easy, to listen to the very unkind comments some people make about us and *their* rea-sons why our husbands/wives have left us. And as those particular people blame us for what has hap-pened, then we take on the guilt as well. Fortunately for most of us, those people are only a handful, and are not the ones we would really want as our friends anyway. The trouble is that these comments have an uncanny way of getting back to us, and then the dam-age is done. And there we are, blaming ourselves again! Guilt, guilt and more guilt!

I want to say a word here about our Christian upbringing – if we've had one. I think there are those types of churchmanship which actually engender guilt in us from day one. We are taught to look at our lives, examine our consciences, and go over our attitudes in detail. The implication being we have 'sinned' or done something wrong. It's another short bus ride to visit this in the area of our personal relationships, and use our 'training' to take the blame. I think at these times it's vitally important to have trusted friends to help us keep things in perspective.

We have looked a little at why women blame other women. And women find it easy to take the blame. We have such a strong maternal, protective urge in us, and it leaps to the defence of our loved one's character. But this may not always be a gender thing. Robert said, as I have already quoted, 'I felt guilty that my lifestyle as a clergyman was largely to blame for things . . .' I think that many men feel like this and blame 'the job'. Robert goes on to say, most movingly, 'I am not sure I did feel guilt. I am by nature a very restrained . . . well-disciplined person. I had to take an awful lot of "flack" from her . . . everything I did was wrong. There was no chance of doing anything right . . . I just had to bear the . . . pain and injustice with a cast iron stoicism.'

Brenda felt guilty at 'not being able to cope'. I wonder why – I wonder if others helped her to feel this.

Christine says of guilt '. . . I do feel guilty about the "fall out" on my children, particularly our youngest who was little at the time.'

I felt guilty about my children too. Guilty that, as their mother, I could not protect them from the results of their father's actions. Yet there was absolutely *nothing* I could do to stop him leaving. It is so difficult to weed out false guilt from real guilt, especially for Christians. A good friend of mine, a retired Christian GP, who has seen plenty of hurting Christians (in every way!), said to me, 'Emotions are a F.A.G. Fear, Anger,

70

Guilt!' How true, but what energy we use on them. Either experiencing them, or trying to suppress them.

While we are on 'little' words . . .! We need to learn the meaning of the words real . . . human . . . honesty . . . reality . . . and openness. We need to learn how not to give in to pressure to have a 'big smile, and a big Bible'! There is nothing wrong with a big Bible – as long as we don't hide behind it. Or maybe if we do peep out we may be suffering from 'SWEG' (with apologies to the evangelicals!). 'SWEG' is a 'Sickly Sweet Evangelical Grin!' I think that most of us can identify with that. I know we can't go round looking sad, miserable and careworn all the time. But neither can we grin our way through heartache and bereavement. We've all been to meetings where the leader, or members of the singing group, or any others there, are grinning from ear to ear the whole time. Singing lustily, hands held high. Lovely – if it's genuine. I'm sure many times it is. I'm equally as sure sometimes it isn't. How many of those people go home to empty flats, empty lives, and empty hearts? How many just make it round the corner after the meeting before breaking down and letting out deep feelings of suppressed hurt? I wonder.

I think for some of us, we may feel more guilty if our spouses cannot handle *their* guilt. Then, they may create a story which may have elements of the truth in it, but to make their guilt easier to live with, they have distorted several aspects of it. Usually pretty key aspects, to make adultery more 'understandable'. Such as, 'Well, we weren't really happy', or worse, 'Gill, Jean, Martin, John wasn't happy.' Even if this is true, it still has nothing to do with adultery. Nothing has. Only sin. If it is *not* true, then it is, to say the least, very unkind. It is a projection of their guilt on to us, and it is extremely easy to take that blame. Facts become conveniently rearranged. Different emphases are put on things. Sometimes it is just pure lies. When it happens, it hurts. But it has to be recognised for what it is.

71

Projected guilt from someone else. Recognising it and naming it does an awful lot to diffuse its power over us.

I can almost hear people saying, 'Well, maybe these people who have failed marriages *do* have something to feel guilty about. Maybe they did do something wrong. Maybe they are at fault.' Undoubtedly we do have things to feel guilty about. We're human. We probably failed our spouses in many different ways. Almost certainly we did do something wrong. Probably lots of things if we're honest. I know I did. And I certainly was at fault, not once, but many times.

Sometimes I did any one of the following: I flew off the handle; I was unkind; although I always loved, I acted unlovingly; I was impatient; I did not show enough affection; I failed to cherish; I was a pest; I felt ugly; I felt fat and unlovable; I was difficult; I was off-hand and dismissive; many times I forgot things; I got muddled; I shouted; I was stupid; I was jealous; I was irritating; I swore at him; sometimes I was just plain wrong – wrong – wrong. But – none of this, nor all of this, is sufficient reason to commit adultery. Nothing I ever did, or did not do, was sufficient reason for that, because nothing ever is.

Adultery is a murderer. A murderer of marriages which, without it, could have been healed and restored, however broken. Adultery, like bacteria, needs several things to feed it, and like bacteria, it grows and becomes big frighteningly fast. It needs deceit, it needs lies, it needs broken promises and wrong intents. It needs lust and self deception, it needs sublimation of the truth, and false promises of happiness and satisfaction. It is insidious and persuasive. It invades happiness and corrupts it. It destroys contentment, and turns Christian values on their heads. It distorts vision, and believe me, it is utterly, utterly relentless.

Rob Parsons, Director of CARE For The Family,

writer and international speaker on, among other things, Christian marriage, says, 'Adultery begins with the eyes'. He then goes on to explain that once we give in to what our eyes tell us looks good, we think maybe just maybe . . .? And then we are lost, and it is all as unstoppable as the tide, unless we keep our eyes on the Father of Truth. Adultery is one of the biggest killers of happiness and destroyer of lives that we have in our society today. It always has been – it's just that now it's more talked about. Those of us who have suffered as a result of it must differentiate between taking the blame for what we did wrong in our marriages, and making that blame the reason for our spouse's infidelity, and thus accepting the guilt for the affair.

In his excellent book *Loving Against The Odds*, Rob Parsons writes, 'The tragedy about the affair is that it has the ability to make everybody feel responsible for it – except the people who are involved in it. It's not at all uncommon to hear children say "If we'd been better behaved Dad wouldn't have gone", or to hear a husband or wife torment themselves about their past mistakes.'[5]

I am sure I am not alone when I say that I have had a pretty interesting time trying to cope with the 'variations on a theme' which have filtered through to me, about the reasons why my husband left me. Many things about my marriage I am proud of. Some things, I bitterly regret. But I feel no guilt for his adultery. That step has been a hard journey, but I'm glad I made it. At times though I'm sure we all feel like I did when I wrote the following:

No Beautiful Thoughts

No 'beautiful thoughts' today Lord.
Just an overwhelming sense
of failure in this situation
– of helplessness
– of inadequacy.
A sense of being totally unable
to handle it
– alone.

Come in Lord Jesus, and make something
of this miserable heap.

Chapter Five

'FEELINGS CHRISTIANS 'SHOULDN'T' HAVE (II)

ANGER AND FEAR

See your anger child
Face the lion within
Look up
See my hands reaching down
Place in them, your anger.

For see child
It fits my wounds
So perfectly.

I drove home that day absolutely shaking with anger.
When I reached my flat, I paced round the lounge like
a caged tiger. I wanted to cry to gain some relief, but I
felt too angry. Whilst I love being outside, I am not in
any way a walker. I have always regarded God's gift of
two legs as being one for the brake, and one for the
accelerator – so I couldn't even walk off my fury! I
wanted to run though, to run and run over open fields,
until I dropped with exhaustion. Instead I sat down at
my piano and murdered several pieces of Chopin, and
a few 'Songs of Fellowship' just for good measure!

What had made me so angry? Very little really. I felt
that someone who really mattered to me had just over-
looked one of my needs – a pretty important need, it
has to be said. I had driven away from their flat steam-

ing! After my piano playing episode, I calmed down and thought rather more rationally about what had just happened. I recognised that I had felt disproportionately angry to how I had just been treated. The force of my feelings had shaken me, until I realised that this was a case of displaced anger. When we have been hurt badly by another person, and especially if we also feel we have been misunderstood, we need to be able to recognise what I call D.A.S. – Displaced Anger Syndrome. If we don't, we may find ourselves in deep trouble, and wondering what on earth is going on in our lives.

Displaced anger is real anger. It is not the emotion of anger which is displaced, but where we are directing it. We all know this type of scenario.

Malcolm has had a really dreadful day at the office, because someone has pulled out of an important deal at the last minute. This means weeks of staying late at the office, and lots of hard work being wasted. He is furious. The coffee arrives three minutes late because Cath, the coffee lady, had a dentist appointment, and the dentist kept her waiting. Malcolm lets rip at Cath, venting much of his pent up fury about the failed deal on to her. She doesn't know what on earth is up with him as he's usually very friendly, so she takes it out on her friend Gloria, who has used Cath's mop to clean up a spillage in the canteen. Gloria in turn, launches into Alice, the cook, who has just told her, 'No, you can't have a cheese salad for lunch, because we're fresh outta cheese!' A decidedly peeved Alice is extremely rude to Ollie, the tall friendly bus conductor, because the bus is five minutes late. It's not Ollie's fault London traffic is so dreadful, so he goes home and kicks the cat. All I can say after all that displaced anger is, if you're a mouse – hide!

See what I mean? Displaced – and disproportionate anger at really very small things. Normally Malcolm would have commiserated with Cath about the coffee, and they would have had a joint moan about dental fees! And Cath would not usually mind Gloria using her mop – she would have teased her about being clumsy. On a normal day, Gloria would have told Alice that cheese is fattening anyway, and she'd rather have a tuna salad. Alice, in turn, usually joined Ollie in a friendly grumble about the state of the capital's traffic. Ollie's cat would not feel like a good case for the R.S.P.C.A., and the mouse would be safe – well, safer anyway!

Malcolm would have been far better if he had gone out for a round of golf, or dug his garden for an hour, or even mown the lawn or cleaned the car! Negative feelings of anger can be turned into positive feelings if we do something to dissipate them. By using hard physical energy we get our anger out. And that is what we need to do. If it stays inside us, every time something else happens on top of it, it goes a little deeper. Buried anger is BIG TROUBLE! It can explode at any moment, or it can, if left buried long enough, turn to depression. It is essential regularly to 'empty our accounts' of anger, or later we shall have an overdraft of problems on our hands.

We all visit things or feelings from other situations on to now. The first situation may be a long time ago – many years in some cases. It may be relatively recently. Sometimes we may know exactly what it is that is making us feel so angry. Sometimes we don't – we only know *something* is. There are times when we can recognise the original source of the anger. Doing that and owning it can often be enough to diffuse it to an appropriate degree for the present situation. We may need help to trace the origins of deep seated or consuming anger. I am not necessarily advocating everyone trotting off, cheque book in hand, to their local psychoanalyst every time they feel angry! But for some of us, we may need to admit that there is a huge 'lion within', who roars at the wrong times, and in the wrong places.

We may need to be courageous enough to say, 'I need help in finding my lion a suitable home.' I know I did, and although it was very difficult at times, painful and disturbing at others, and occasionally all three at once, my lion within sleeps the more peacefully, because I am learning when to let him out of his cage more appropriately.

Obviously abandonment can trigger many past angers, and disturb any 'lions within'. If someone has been bullied at school and treated unfairly, it can resonate into a failed marriage. Survivors of sexual, physical, or mental abuse always feel great anger at the way they have been treated by another person or persons. For anyone being abandoned, abused or badly treated by a spouse, it can release enormous anger from these earlier betrayals. Some may have felt the least loved sibling in a family, or the least clever one, and their lions roar powerfully indeed when yet another important person in their lives says, 'I do not want you. I do not love you. You do not matter to me. I do not care.'

If the marriage ending is a mutual decision, as opposed to one party's desertion, there may well be enormous anger with each other. Each may feel furious that the other could not meet their needs, or did not understand them. They may feel angry with themselves as not 'making a success' of their marriage.

For Christians there is the added dimension of being angry with God. Why didn't He intervene? Why didn't He answer my prayers? Why did He let my husband/wife give in to the wiles of someone else?

Brenda says, 'I felt very angry with the two people concerned, even to the extent of wanting to do them physical harm. I was also angry with God at seeming not to answer my prayers . . . Sometimes I denied the anger, but mainly I allowed it to surface and went and kicked a tree!'

Sometimes it can take us years to acknowledge that

we are angry at all, never mind thinking about caged lions within! This was true for Christine. She says, 'Only recently have I acknowledged that I did, and do feel angry.' (This is after a space of several years.)

Others may be able to handle their anger in different ways. Robert says, 'I am the sort of person who is disciplined about my emotions. Yes, I was very hurt and angry, at times. However, I ease my emotions safely and slowly by a controlled grip on myself. Rather like controlling a heavy weight by means of a hawser round a bollard . . . if you see what I mean.'

For myself, my anger only came much later, after the initial numbness had worn off – and when I more fully realised all I had to cope with because of my husband's desertion. The second time he left me, I was, though still tremendously shocked, far angrier at first. I knew so much more, all that would be involved and all I would have to go through. I had, after all, had a dummy run.

Elizabeth, who tells her story in Chapter Eleven, felt anger later on too, but especially so at the time her husband left, because her children were only tiny. She says, 'I did not feel at all angry at first, I just felt numb and helpless to prevent what was happening to us as a family. But gradually as the depth of his deceit and betrayal of trust unfolded, one of my emotions was anger. At times I felt deeply angry, especially when I thought of my children, who were very young, and so dependent and vulnerable. How could he leave them?'

I identify with that, even though my daughters were much older the second time my husband left. I felt angry that the one person in the world who should have been protecting us all, was devastating my 'children', and preventing me from protecting them against his actions. I was being stopped from exercising to the full my role as a mother. My protective instinct was being frustrated. It has been one of my greatest agonies to watch my daughters suffer, and be helpless to prevent it. Their pain has torn the heart out of me, and if it would have eased their grief, I would have walked through fire and over broken glass for them. It made me so angry on their behalf, and it was and still is, totally incomprehensible to me, how a parent can inflict so much pain on their children, just because of something *they* want for themselves. And it is no excuse to say, 'Well, they're older now and they'll cope. These things happen and they're very resilient.' Older does not mean less pain – these things shouldn't happen – and as for resilience, who can say what scars are left after such a betrayal? Unless the parent concerned is violent or abusive, parental desertion, whatever the age of the children, *always* causes heartache, it *always* scars them, and amongst other things, it usually damages their ability to trust people.

In marriage breakdown of course, the situation goes on. We stay without our absent spouses. That life is gone – forever. We cannot stay at the same level of anger, or we will end up destroying ourselves. Elizabeth puts this very well, 'My situation is going on, so yes, I do sometimes feel angry, but to a much lesser degree and not over the same things. My anger has never been an isolated emotion. I think that initially anger can be a good thing, as it can keep a person going, carries them through, but to stay angry for too long can be very destructive. At one stage the anger I felt was a real problem in my moving forward, but I wanted my children and myself to survive and wanted to stop feeling so angry and move on with my life, as anger can trap you in the past. The children and I needed to be able to live with hope and enjoyment in the present and look forward to our future. Having said this, I couldn't and didn't try to force my anger to go, but there did seem to be a natural progression through which I passed and am now moving on in my life. I do what I can about the things I can influence and those I cannot I try not to dwell on. I'm getting more and more successful at this!'

Brenda, on the other hand, writes movingly about her thoughts and feelings on anger; 'I do not feel angry today. Just a very deep sadness at what appears to have been wasted years, both in our relationship before he left, and to a lesser degree, since he went.'

I feel that too. Deep sadness for all the lost opportunities – all the missed chances – all the fun and happiness that could have been. The happy marriage that was blossoming from, yes, heartache and deceit, but also from so many years of shared memories – family holidays, births, deaths, proud moments for our children, secrets shared together that no one else knew about, intimate nicknames, all the shared fun and being together that makes a marriage what it is. Out of all this, after my husband came back, was coming an even better relationship, the possibility of *real* openness and honesty, of continued shared ministry, of passion and companionship, slipping into the sharing of our golden years together. Sometimes I feel an almost unbearable sadness that all this was snatched away, but I feel anger too. Anger that all this could be trampled on with size ten boots of insensitivity and a *massive* selfishness which sees another's spouse and says; 'I want, therefore I will have' – no matter what the cost to the wife/husband, or the children of that marriage.

Brenda put this so very well, after her husband had visited her. 'Eventually he came, and he brought her with him! I was able to keep from physical violence only in Your strength Lord. I wanted to kill her, to hurt her as she was hurting me. The worst of all was to see them holding hands, embracing each other. Suddenly I felt so much anger. How dare they do this in front of me. They see no sin in what they are doing. She seems to think that she has a right to steal my husband, although she has a husband of her own.'

Of *her* present anger, Christine says simply, 'I cope with the anger by admitting it and allowing myself to feel it.'

Robert speaks of how his faith has helped him to deal with his anger, 'I am bound to say . . . it is my faith that has taken the strain. I would say it was the "bollard" around which I eased my pain and anguish . . . it can take the strain . . .'

Yes, it can take the strain. So can bashing a pillow, ruining Chopin on the piano, running, shouting, talking with a friend, frantically cleaning the house, painting, playing golf, walking the dog – anything which involves using physical energy. Sometimes we need to *do* something to help us get our anger out. It may be listening to soothing music, or it may be throwing plates at a wall, but we must recognise the need to do something physical as an aid to expressing our anger.

But we can also tell God about it. We can tell Him how furious we are, with whom, why, and to what degree. We don't even need to be polite! He is after all, big enough to take our anger. Pour it all out to Him. Yell, 'God, I feel so angry because . . .', or if that's too complicated, 'God, I feel so angry', or even 'God, God, help me . . .' He will. And it's O.K. to do this – I promise.

But it's all right to feel angry *with* God, as well as at Him. Of course we're furious with God sometimes. He's infinite. We're finite. It's only by His grace that the two ever meet. When we don't understand something, it can make us angry. It's human nature. He knows, He's been there, done that, and got the tee-shirt and the mug of humanity! We are almost sure to feel angry with God. And DON'T WORRY! Others may not understand this – but HE DOES! I have felt irate with Him. I still do on occasions. How can we help it, if all we've done is to stay faithful to Him, to our marriage vows, to our husbands/wives, and we're left alone, in bad emotional pain, while they appear to be 'living the life of Riley' with someone else?

I do not deny my wrath. I may try to understand it, but I do not deny it. I tell God about it, even if it feels directed at Him. That is what He has asked me to do. You see, He wants our honesty so much more than our denial of emotions. Honesty is the solution which washes the blame out of the anger we lift openly to, and at, Him. Psalm Four says, 'Be angry, but sin not. Commune with your heart on your bed and be silent.' Maybe a modern translation of that could be: '*Feel* your anger, but don't let it lead you into doing wrong. Think about it carefully, and don't swear at others because of it.' But we are usually unable to solve problems all alone. I can almost see, as I write, two open, wounded hands, stretching out towards me saying, 'Little one, give your anger to me. It fits my wounds so perfectly.'

Of course, there are those whose rage at their marriage breakdown, or at being abandoned, is just that. We do not all have 'skeletons in our cupboards'. I would be the last one to presume to disagree with anyone who said their anger was solely to do with the present. I would not gravely shake my head, and tell them that past anger is being suppressed! We have to learn to respect what others say to us – which means accepting it, even if we disagree. Of course, in a counselling situation, these dynamics are rather different, but in ordinary conversation, if someone says that is how it is for them, then that is how it is for them. Because *they* say so. I sometimes get fed up with people telling me what I *really* mean, or think, or even worse, what I feel, because the other person in the conversation is not really listening to what I have said, or doesn't agree with me.

But for all of us, I think we need to remember D.A.S. There are frequent occasions in which I have felt disproportionately angry in a given situation. Like the time my car suddenly cut out completely on a dark windy road in the town where I live. It was a very isolated road, and as it was also very late, I was extremely frightened, and cross. I found myself shouting at the car, but then I went on, '. . . and I wouldn't be in this frightful situation if he hadn't gone. I wouldn't be driving this car. I wouldn't live in this town. And I certainly wouldn't be out on this dark and windy road at this hour, alone, and terrified!' I was, without realising it, verbalising my D.A.S.! To be honest, I was also furious with myself because I had not sorted out getting a mobile 'phone. An omission which was hastily redressed after that night! That was something positive and tangible I could do about a situation which caused me both anger and fear. Now I drive at night, with a mind much at ease, because of my little black telephone beside me in the car. I do not think I shall get that angry again in a similar situation.

But I *have* found that when I start to feel angry, I need to be very aware of the cause of it. If I stop and do a rapid check, it helps tremendously. It probably means the rest of the population are much safer too!

But in the car on that dark night, I was not only angry, I was afraid too. Actually then, with very good reason. But what about fear, when we suddenly find ourselves alone? Looking back, there were so many things which made me fearful when my husband left. He had always been there to lean on. Now, he was gone. There were so many things that made me afraid, that I almost became afraid of fear itself.

I became afraid of the future. I had no home – no town, no money. Where would I live? How could I possibly afford to live? I was scared of not being able to support myself. I had not worked full time for over twenty years. I was afraid for the girls. How would they handle again, the destruction of their secure and safe home life? The second time my husband left me, I was terrified of being alone – all alone, as both the girls were living and working in London by that time. How would I cope with a tiny, empty flat, instead of a big, bustling, busy vicarage? I was afraid of never being useful. Would I ever again be able to exercise any meaningful ministry? I was fearful of the distant future. No pension, no insurance, no monetary help of any kind for all the future I could see. Absolutely *no* financial security. All gone – in a day. What would happen when I became too old to work? And maybe, worst of all, I was afraid of myself. Who was I now? I had lost *everything*. Role, ministry, position. I was a wanderer, with no home, and no town. I felt barely alive, and it felt completely and utterly terrifying. I used to say to God, 'Lord, who am I? Please show me myself.' Now that may seem a pretty sensible thing to pray in the light of what I've said. Let me hastily add a warning here! Sensible . . . Um . . . Understandable? . . . maybe . . . Dangerous . . . YES, YES, YES! When I asked God 'Who am I, Lord?' He took all the shredded parts of my life, mixed it all up, and turned it inside out! He does that kind of thing! Beware!

After I had found a new town, a new home, a new church, new friends, new interests, new ministry, after He had started 'making all things new', He then – well, if *felt* like, He picked up the book, and threw it at me! I seemed to really 'go through the mill', and had to battle with so many things. But slowly, painfully, at *my* speed, He is answering my heartfelt prayer 'Who am I, Lord?' some days, I still wonder, but at least now, I know that He knows, and is unfolding the canvas at a speed slow enough for me to take in the picture.

Again, like my anger, I do not deny my fears. I tell Him of course, but I also speak to friends. God has a great way of speaking to us through friends. He valued so much the friendship of the disciples, and I value so much my many friends, with whom I share this journey called 'life'.

Some of our fears we can actually *do* something about. Like my mobile 'phone. Some, we cannot. Those are the ones we need to learn to live with. I can hear someone saying, 'Give your fears to God.' Would that it were that simple. There is the little problem of our humanity, which has an annoying habit of getting in the way! Some may feel this is 'lack of faith' – I don't think it is. Living by faith for *everything*, job, money, health, enough energy to cope with a life that demands too much, courage to go on – well, it has to be experienced to be believed. One thing I *do* know. God, my God, is God of the darkness as well as the light. He understands my fears. He does not accuse me of possessing a 'spirit of fear'. Instead He says to me, 'Daughter, come. Your fears are so heavy. See, place your hands, so full of fear, in mine. That way, I can help you to carry it.' I know the more I do that, the more of the burden He will carry. What none of us needs is people making us feel guilty, because we are honest enough to say that sometimes we are afraid. What we *do* need is to hear Him say directly, or through friends, as He does, 'I understand.'

Fear has to be addressed. It has to be looked at. But for those of us, in our sometimes frightening lives, more than anything else, it has to be lived with, on a daily basis, as our situations continue unchanged.

Brenda expressed her fears this way, 'I was fearful of being alone, no physical presence on arriving home to an empty house. Although I knew God was with me, the loneliness was overpowering. Today, things are a lot better, but I am still worried (perhaps not as strong as fearful) about coping alone for the rest of my life.'

Christine sums up the fear which many of us feel, 'I am afraid of a lonely/impoverished old age.'

For Elizabeth, with very much younger children, her fears are different. She is afraid that '. . . the children would feel unloved and rejected by their father.'

In the end, of course, we all have fears with which we have to battle. Some will not acknowledge them, thus giving in to another fear. The fear of being afraid. 'I trust God for everything.' Brilliant! Could you please put pen to paper, telling the rest of us how to do it?!

When you are worn, and hurting, the road seems to stretch endlessly ahead. I would much rather look up and say, 'God, I want to trust You completely. I can only do that by telling You that I am tired and at times dispirited. Sometimes I feel angry, and sometimes afraid, and sometimes, both. But most of all, I want to tell You that I love You, and I know how very much You love me.' I just know He smiles.

In the Secret Places

In the secret places
in the hidden parts, my Saviour
in every space
– there is pain

In every cell
each thought
each whispered prayer
– I hurt.
Most words that are spoken to me
feel like nails
driven into
my outstretched hands.

I cannot free them
to let them cover my heart
– I cannot push away
this agony.

My feet too, my Saviour
are nailed –
nailed to the path
that I must walk.

My side hurts too
where the sword pierced deep
– and with each new thrust

it bleeds again.
The tears I shed
are tears of blood, my Saviour
– as each new thorn
is woven into my crown.

And I have no words that I can say
– my lips must stay closed
– for there is no one
to listen.

And once again, my Saviour
in every space
each hidden part
– there is pain.

As my head drops with weariness
I look down
into the loving face
of Mary.

Our Lady too, is weeping
Our Lady too, is silent
– but she is there
and she waits patiently.

Her side too, is pierced
her heart too, is bound
– but with her nailed hands
she lifts my head
and points
– to You.

And in the sweat
the noise – the fear –
the agony of my life
– as I look at You
I see You looking at me –
it is enough, my Saviour
– it is enough for me.

Chapter Six

FEELINGS CHRISTIANS 'SHOULDN'T' HAVE (III)

ANXIETY AND DOUBT

Everyone worries, and everyone has doubts of one kind or another. I do not think it is a sin to worry, or to have doubts. Worries are natural if we have lost everything – spouse, sometimes home, town, church, role and security. Doubts make us question, and usually grow, through questioning, into certainties.

Recently I heard a Bishop announce from a pulpit: 'I want to talk to those who have committed the sins of worry and doubt.' I felt shattered, but angry too. I knew I was not the only one in the church that day who at various times in my life, had wrestled with doubt. Whilst I respect the priesthood very much, I do not think Bishops are infallible, and I felt for all of us who have been honest enough to own up to doubts of one kind or another. I knew there were those in the church that day, who would have a layer of guilt added to their anxieties and doubts simply because of what a Bishop had said.

In Luke chapter 12, verses 22 to 30, Jesus does indeed tell us not to worry. '. . . And so I tell you not to worry about the food you need to stay alive or about the clothes you need for your body. Life is much more important than food, and the body much more important than clothes.'

But He does not say this because to worry is a sin.

He says this because He loves us so much that He does not want us to wear ourselves out with anxieties. When we suffer in any way, He grieves with us, and He suffers too. When we are abandoned or deserted, or our marriage collapses, His heart is broken too, and for every tear we weep, He weeps deeply with us and for us. In verses 25 and 26 of Luke 12, it says: 'Can any of you live a bit longer by worrying about it? If you can't manage even such a small thing, why worry about the other things?'

Jesus knows that the energy put into worrying is wasted, and He wants to spare us the angst of it. But it is not a sin. In verse 32 of the same chapter, He goes on to say: 'Do not be afraid, little flock, for your Father is pleased to give you the kingdom.' Can you not hear the love in His voice, and feel the smile on His face as He says this to us? And 'little flock' is a term of endearment. He is assuring us that though we do worry (and He knows we will, or He would not have said any of this in the first place) it actually achieves nothing. But in His enormous forgiving love for us, He wants to assure us that even if we do worry, 'Our Father is pleased to give us the kingdom.' He is telling us that our worrying cannot remove from us the things of eternity, but for our sakes, He would rather we save ourselves the grief of anxiety. Very few people in all honesty, can trust God one hundred per cent all the time. Jesus is only urging us to try. What He does not want us to do is to sit and worry, because we are anxious or feel doubts about some things, for thus it becomes a vicious circle.

When we are left alone, we may become worried about many different things – or previous certainties become frightening and uncertain doubts.

Christine's main worry was: 'Coping with the stress of life with no help or support. It was a bit like a bad dream after all. We had expected to spend the rest of our lives with our spouses, and had not ever thought about suddenly having to handle *everything* alone.'

Elizabeth's concerns were for her children: 'I was worried about becoming ill long term – who will look after the children? Loneliness too, but this fear is now much less. Making decisions on my own. The children's happiness, and providing for day to day living. The lack of short and long term financial security – providing for my children and myself.'

Even though Robert's children were much older than Elizabeth's at the time of the breakdown, he says: 'My main concern over the breakdown of the marriage was my children. The effect that it would have on them. Two children, two boys, were in their late teens, and were very good. My daughter in her early teens, was far more of a worry. As it was Janet and I were very much in agreement on the fact that we should continue our mutual care of the children. There was no dispute here, and we were able to work responsibly with them. I am glad to report that this has worked out well. Now they are in their late twenties and early thirties, and we do have very good family relationships of an adult nature. Sadly, I feel my experience has left them all "marriage shy". . .'

It is so natural to worry, isn't it? Even the disciples did it, and they had Jesus with them physically. They were frantic with worry when they had a huge hungry crowd on their hands. They were worried when Jesus told them to open Lazareth's tomb, when He went to eat with tax collectors and sinners, when they saw He was determined to go to Jerusalem and about providing for their families when they were unable to catch any fish. And after His arrest, they were worried beyond belief that they might be recognised as Jesus' followers.

I believe all worry stems from a fear of not being in control. If things in our lives are not under our control, then they control us, and not the other way around. If we are being controlled, then we feel helpless, or vic-

tims, or both. If the disciples had been unable to control
the crowds, then the crowds would very soon have
controlled them! They were not in control of a dead
body in a tomb, they had no idea what was about to
happen – if Jesus got too friendly with undesirables,
then they could easily end up (or so *they* thought) controlling Jesus – and them! They certainly did not feel in
control at the thought of Him going to Jerusalem and
facing all those angry Roman soldiers – anything could
happen! They felt helpless too, when they could not
catch any fish; for even though mortgages were different then, it still meant they had financial commitments
to meet to provide for their families. It was, after all, the
same in those days as it is now. No money – no food!
And they could most definitely see their lives spiralling
uncontrollably at the thought of being accused of being
one of Jesus' followers. They could very clearly see
themselves being put on trial, then condemned to
prison or death – all at the control of other people. No
wonder they were worried!

It is, quite simply, human nature to worry. I know
we are trying to overcome our nature, and become
more like God, but in the meantime we have to live
with our humanity. This is not defeatism – it is not giving in to it and saying, 'Oh well, it's too hard – let it all
just hang out!' We cannot deny our humanity. Being
told it is a sin to worry is, in my book, almost tanta-
mount to a sin in itself. Christ is the only person who
did not worry, as we know it. There were definitely
times when He did feel anxious. In the garden of
Gethsemane He said: 'Father . . . my Father! All things
are possible for you. Take this cup of suffering away
from me . . .' (Mark chapter 14, verse 36).

We can get into such a state that we begin to worry
because we are worrying! Add a layer of guilt on to all
that, and we end up feeling pretty grotty! I think it is
far better to say, openly to God, that yes, we *do* worry,
and yes, we wish we didn't, but would He please take

our worries and concerns, and help us to bear them. I think that, for me, is the only prayer I can make completely honestly. It's no good our saying to God: 'God, please help me not to worry, thank you.' Then get up from our knees, with all the same problems still there, and know that He can actually see straight through us. He knows our thoughts before we think them. We can only tell God how it is for us. We can pretend, but it serves absolutely no purpose. Except to give us a headache!

I have found that God does take me at my word. It isn't that I don't know He can lift the worries away completely. I know He can. But I also know that I won't let Him! He understands that, and He has a wonderful way of easing them just enough for me to take. Some of the problems have been, and still are, pretty big. Homeless, townless, penniless, with no role, no identity, jobless, and with no tangible future, all I *could* do was to lean onto Him. And I did. It felt good, and in the middle of the dreadful pain, life felt, at the same time in the darkest hours, like a long hug from God. I knew with all my heart that He held me. But I also knew I had two broken-hearted daughters to care for, and I knew however bad I felt, I could not just sit down under it and moan about how unfair life was, even though it was – grossly! 'Hand all your cares to Him.' Sure, I did. But He did not take them away. Until each problem was solved, like finding a home, town, job, church, He helped me to carry them.

I was afraid of losing control of my life. I had, after all, been put in this position by others, and I was completely vulnerable. I think a lot of people who have been deserted, especially if it meant losing their home and everything I did, will agree with me when I say I did not begin to feel at all better until I had regained at least a little control of my life. I remember standing in my new flat, feeling scared yes, but at least feeling that this was *my* space. Here I could do what *I* wanted to do.

Here I was not constantly anxious about being in some-one else's home. Here I did not feel awkward or a nui-sance.

For each of us there will be different things that worry us. I have been amazed at the way some of my friends have coped with huge worries at a time when their lives were in shreds – then seen them fall apart at a seemingly tiny little thing, which to me has seemed nothing to worry about at all! I know that some of my anxieties have seemed stupid to other people, but it hasn't stopped me worrying just because they could not understand my concern. Now, if any one says to me: 'Sue, I'm really worried about so and so – do you know what I mean?' – if I do know, I say so. If I don't know what they mean, I will say, 'Well, I can see it's causing you great concern, and that's what matters.'

So let's not tie ourselves in knots about worry. We all do it. And as we remember Christ's words, not to worry, let us not go away and worry because we can't stop worrying! What a spiral of wasted energy!

I think one thing that makes Christians worry almost more than anything, is doubts about their faith. I also think this is something we have imposed on our-selves. I am sure that Jesus never laid into the disciples because they had doubts. He did tell Peter to keep his eyes on Him when he was sinking in the waves, but He didn't spend ages telling him how dreadful he was because he had doubted.

We may have doubts about any aspect of our faith, or we may have doubts about the whole. Usually doubts grow through questioning into certainties, but they can be very distressing when they happen. Sometimes we can be fearful that our faith will not stand up to the test. Brenda says: 'My faith has, on the whole, remained strong. On some occasions I became, and still continue to become, fearful of my faith reced-ing. But as this has not happened so far, I am hanging in there.'

Sometimes doubts are brought on by weariness and fatigue. Elizabeth says: 'I sometimes have doubts about my faith and ability to cope as a one parent family, especially on those days when I feel so exhausted. And I've asked God if He really is there on occasions, but I know He is. He says to me, 'Yes, I am. I love you and your children, I care. You cannot see my whole plan, but I will be with you.'

Christine, on the other hand, says: 'My faith deserted me after the break-up, due, I suspect, to my deep and prolonged depression. As I could not reach out to other people, so I could not feel the presence of God.'

Robert's experience was totally the opposite to this. 'The whole experience was, I am bound to say, faith enriching. Constant prayer . . . hours and hours . . . I am fortunate in having a lovely church to pray in. What a lovely place to withdraw into . . . time and again. In the heat of misery and pain . . . you are not concerned about being thoughtful about your faith. You just want to be there with God. You just want Him to sort things out . . . you come in bruised in heart, raging in mind, protesting, exhausted, low and surrounded by blackness, busted, exasperated. Yet, the familiar seat, the familiar setting, the space, the cool, the still, the gentleness, the totally unthreatening, unhurtful place, unchanged in centuries, open and there for you. It's . . . your burrow . . . into the warm earth which gave you life in the first place, it's your grave, tranquil and unmoving. It's the place where God may give you resurrection for a few more days.

'A space, a beautiful space, where new life, new energy, new insights which enable you to do all the ducking and diving in domestic strife you may have to do.

'It is not a matter of knowing, or believing, it is simply a matter of using the faith because over the past years you have mysteriously been given it. Faith is an instinct

... to cope with life ... in a spiritual way, given by God.'

It is not like that for everyone though, and if we do have doubts it is essential that we feel we can seek help. This can be from a trusted friend, or an older Christian. It may be our priest, or vicar. It may be a respected counsellor. Someone whose opinion we value, and whose judgement we trust. We may not feel able to read huge books on the subject of doubt – I think conversation is better anyway, because we need dialogue, an answer, a 'prod' to help us try to sort out our doubts and certainties.

For myself, I must be honest and say that although I have had doubts about many things, I have never had doubts about my faith. It seemed the most natural thing in the world to turn to Him when life went pear shaped! For me He was, and still is on some days, my only certainty. I knew He would not let me down. I knew this because of my knowledge of Him in the past.

I looked back over my life and saw the evidence. It was very clear to me that He had been in my life all the way through. I suppose the last time my husband left me it was easier to look back and see His hand at work, because I had the evidence of the first time to go on. However it was also much more difficult, because it hurt so very much more. But something happened to me before the first time my husband left, which showed me beyond doubt that God was in the whole story, as it were, and I was completely overwhelmed. I would like to recount what happened.

Before I found out about the first affair, but when I knew something was wrong with my husband, God drew me to Himself in a very special way. I used to go out into the orchard in the vicarage garden each day, and spend time just being with Him. I remember it felt, on these occasions, that earth and heaven were very near, and it felt a privilege to be there. I had the strongest feeling of God holding me close, but also that in some way I did not understand, I was 'holding my breath'. I just enjoyed those very special times, and continued to wait.

But alongside this, every time I went to the Eucharist – every time I made my Communion, if my husband was celebrating, something very strange happened. I was of course, receiving the chalice and the wafer from his hands. Every time it came to the chalice being held out to me by *him*, I had the strongest picture imprinted on my mind. His hands were holding the cup out to me, but instead of the stem of the chalice, under his hands, this had become a sword which he held above my head. Week after week this happened. It troubled me very much, but I did not know what to do about it. In the end I told my spiritual director about it, and he said: 'Draw the picture.' So I did, and as I drew it, I found myself writing the words that Simeon had spoken to Mary in the Temple, when she and Joseph had presented Jesus for circumcision: 'And a sword will pierce your heart also.' I did not know at the time, but my spiritual director knew about my husband's affair, but he was practising 'the seal of the confessional', and there was no way he could tell me. He must of course have realised what the picture and the words meant, and I will never forget the long measuring look he gave me when I showed him the drawing. Both the picture and the words continued until after the eruption in my life, and then they ceased as suddenly as they had begun.

Many months later, after I had experienced some of the horrors which desertion and abandonment bring, my Oblate Sister gave me the following words, written by the poet Elizabeth Jennings.[6]

In Christ's Place

You will be crucified for me
You will be hunted in the place
You thought most safe. And you will see

> *The darkness on a threatener's face*
> *Then hear the shouts of Calvary*
> *And learn the opposite of peace*
>
> *My temple is not safe from this*
> *Remember I was angry there*
> *And can be now in silences.*
> *This is the sword I told you of*
> *Which strikes most deeply where there's love.*

I was both stunned and comforted by these words. God had showed me that a sword would indeed pierce my heart, as it had Mary's. And more than that, the picture showed me so clearly the sword being held in my husband's hands. I was hunted, by that group of 'friends' in the place I thought most safe – church. And I certainly saw the darkness on their faces as they told me I was 'tainted by my husband's sin'. I really did feel as if I was being crucified, both by my husband, and by them, and I definitely 'learnt the opposite of peace'. The sword struck most deeply because my heart was full of love for the person who wielded it.

I realised that all those special times, all that drawing me close to Him, was in preparation, and the picture was both a warning, and God's amazing way of showing me He held me, and knew what I was going through. It was His way of letting me know that although my life was about to become a place of deep and lasting pain, He was still in control of it. He knew that later when my Oblate Sister had given me the poem, I would fully understand the meaning of the vision. I think too, it was His way of showing me He was calling me into 'sharing in the fellowship of His sufferings', for there is a very real way in which Christ asks us to make sense of our suffering, by seeing it as sharing with Him. At the time, it was hard to believe He was taking so much trouble over me, and I began to feel very special to Him, and experience more the depth of His love for us.

Before it happened, I had dreams too. Dreams of being down a deep, dark hole, with my husband standing at the top, looking down at me, but he would not help me climb out of the hole, and in the end he simply walked away. Later, looking back, I did not need a dream analyst to explain the meaning of those dreams!

There is absolutely no way any of us can look back with the knowledge of hindsight and say, 'I would have done that differently.' Well, we can, I suppose, but there is a tremendous amount of energy wasted on 'if onlys'. Lots of us, I know, have been over and over the same thing hundreds and hundreds of times, painting a different scenario in our minds, or replaying certain events. We rewrite the script, saying, 'That was what happened – not that.' But . . . and it's a pretty big 'but', at the end of it all, things are just the same.

Probably when I knew something was wrong with my husband, it would have been one of the very few times in life, when a little more worry might have been constructive. I may have felt pushed into doing something to try and find out what was wrong, and if my increasing suspicions were correct. But at the time I was battling with a huge sense of guilt (false guilt, I hasten to add!) because I was even *having* those suspicions in the first place. And *he* was saying all the time, even though it was manifestly obvious it was not true, that there was nothing wrong and I was told I was 'nagging'. Worry really is a waste of time, but when we are in the grip of it, we simply cannot see the wood for the trees.

I think it is interesting that of the four people who have kindly given their stories for this book, the only one who has not expressed anxiety about loneliness or the future, is Robert. My other three contributors are women. Certainly for myself, I would identify with them. I would place fear of loneliness pretty high on my list, but I would put being worried about the future, and especially long term, even higher.

I could write pages and pages giving all the reasons why we, as Christians, shouldn't worry. I could (I hope!) be very eloquent with words. I am sure, sound very convincing. I could quote Bible verses – mostly out of context, of course – and also quote Christian leaders, far more qualified than me (not that *that* would be difficult!). If I put my mind to it, I might write a thesis on the uselessness of worrying, except I expect it would have a title more like 'A discussion on the inadvisability of severe pontification on certain matters relating to a given event which is in the past now!' I could do all this, even sit down and pray individually with each one of you reading this book, and the plain simple fact is – you would still go away and start worrying again! That is NOT 'lack of faith'. I am not just being clever with words here to avoid facing up to some deep seated lack of ability to trust. I am simply telling it how it is. And no, it's not God's ideal for us, but it is human nature – as it is – in all it's fallenness. He loves us, just as we are!

Now that of course, does not mean that we cannot change. Of course we can, because if we let Him, He does it for us. But it is a simple fact that the first stage to stop worrying is to accept the fact that God loves us exactly as we are, even if we're worrying our insides out. He does not condemn us for it. He sympathises. If we start to fret because we're worried about what He thinks of our anxieties, then we really are on the fast road to nowhere. Rest in His love, worries and all. Nestle, don't wrestle. Tell Him of your inability to stop worrying – and doubting. Ask Him to help, sure, but be content to leave it at that. He is. And above all, remember two things. IT IS NOT A SIN TO WORRY, OR TO DOUBT, AND GOD LOVES AND ACCEPTS YOU EXACTLY AS YOU ARE.

Just before I was left on my own for the final time, I

went away to a Convent to save my sanity, and to try and sort out the agony and nightmare my previously happy life had become since that evil letter had arrived. Cliff – the senior priest in the parish – had arranged it because he and my G.P. were so worried about me.

I was worried, and I doubted. I doubted all sorts of things. Mostly my ability to stay alive, and indeed, my desire to go on living. I doubted my ability to cope again with all the horrors of rejection, and all it meant. I felt I had absolutely no energy, and more than any-thing else, I was desperately, frighteningly tired. In the day, sleep was not a problem – staying awake was! But at night, try as I might, I simply could not sleep. So as always, I wrote.

A small word here about writing. I would advise anyone who is in pain, for whatever reason, to put pen to paper. It does not have to come out as poetry. It does not even have to come out as 'good' prose. It does not even have to make sense. After all, a lot of the time, what is happening to us does not make sense! So write gobbledegook if it helps – write anything – but WRITE! Because to write is to get it out, and it does bring tem-porary release – and *sometimes* unexpected clarity.

I do remember on that night, when I had written this next poem, I then slept. Almost certainly because of the last line. I called it 'Shadowlands', because that is where I felt as though I was.

Shadowlands

*There is no light
only borrowed light
in shadowlands –
if someone else leaves
a door ajar
light peeps through
the tiny crack
otherwise*

– there is no light
in shadowlands.
There is pain
and pain
and more pain
in shadowlands –
a deep twisting hurt
which permeates between body and soul
winding itself around the heart,
to leave one reeling and breathless
– there is only pain
in shadowlands.

Tears too deep for words,
which wring the heart of life
– and yet the knowledge
that they must be wept,
if any consolation is to be found –
but they leave only exhaustion
in their wake –
and a dark aching void,
which some would call a heart –
of yes, there are tears in shadowlands.

To be in shadowlands
is to be torn in two,
and yet stay one –
to twist and turn, and all around
is broken glass –
hands are held out,
giving comfort,
only to slip away again
– and the pain returns
in shadowlands.

And is there no escape?
Into each corner that I look,
hands push back that very thing

102

from which I seek to hide
– to weave its convolutions
round my mind;
there is no rest in shadowlands
for sleep,
that kindly harbinger of oblivion,
is a stranger here.

Yet,
through the agony of the darkness
a shaft of pale light appears –
for Someone has pushed the door –
and into the place of no meaning,
into the confusion,
and the fear,
the eyes are forced to look – and see –
that into shadowlands has fallen
– the gentle shadow of a Cross.

Chapter Seven

FEELINGS CHRISTIANS 'SHOULDN'T' HAVE (IV)

DESPAIR – A PAIN BEYOND BEREAVEMENT

'Hope: to cherish a desire of good with some expectation of fulfilment'

'Despair: to be without hope'

I lay on the hall floor in the vicarage. I found I had curled up into the foetal position. All I knew was that I wanted to be even lower – right under the floor, right in the depths of the earth. Great powerful sobs racked my body. They felt as though they were coming from the very depths of my being. I groaned, then shouted. I couldn't make enough noise. My body felt tight, like a coiled spring. If I had possessed at that time the power of rational thought, I would have realised that I had a splitting headache. I felt the pain inside me would consume and destroy me. The only way I could go on living was somehow to get it outside of my body, my mind and my spirit. At that moment, I knew with everything in me how people can die of a broken heart. I do not know what I would have done if anyone had come to the front door. Luckily no-one did, and the girls were both at school. I felt if I screamed loud enough and long enough, some of the unbearable agony would be forced out of me and I would feel as though I could at least stay alive. How long I lay there I do not know, but the screaming was followed by a great bout of the deepest tears it is possible for anyone to weep. Then I lay, exhausted and spent, with no energy left even to stand.

This experience was one face of despair. It has other faces too. In fact, despair has many faces. Sometimes it is seen as the person who has 'dead' eyes. They may be very quiet and if drawn into a conversation will answer in monosyllables or not at all. They sit and stare into space. Often the person concerned will appear to be functioning quite normally, until suddenly it is obvious that you have 'lost' them. I am thinking of a person I know with a very responsible job who to the outside world is coping very well, but inside he is dying. A short time of one-to-one conversation with him soon shows very clearly that he is in fact, underneath it all, quietly despairing. Any trying to lift him is impossible, because we always seem to end back at a position of hopelessness. Sometimes despair can be manic. The person concerned will literally thrash around – 'lose it' – when control finally slips and they feel they are left with nothing.

Despair has many faces because each of us is different, but the word despair is not a popular word in Christian circles. It is an embarrassing word. It is something Christians 'shouldn't feel'. Christ is our hope, isn't He? So how can we despair? Oh, how I wish it were that simple! Maybe it 'should' be – I really don't know. What I do know is – it isn't. It is absolutely no good at all pretending that Christians do not feel despair. We do, and it's that simple. Sometimes there are those who are so knocked by life, whose self-confidence is so shattered, who have severe financial problems and have other major worries as well, that in the end they just 'sit down under it all'. And who can blame them? Add exhaustion and anxiety to a mountain of very big problems and you have the perfect recipe for despair. A heartening big grin and words that we think sound 'Christian' and 'right' are meaningless in the face of real heartfelt despair. Bible verses mean little at times like this. Even Job said to his so-called 'comforters': 'Honest words are convincing, but you are talking nonsense. You think I am talking nothing but wind. Then why do you answer my words of despair?'(Job 6 verses 25 and 26) In other words, 'if you are incapable of hearing what I am saying, then shut up! Don't try to answer me if you haven't really understood what I'm feeling.' Job then goes on to give a very eloquent description of what it feels like to live with severe ongoing emotional pain. 'Human life is like forced army service, like a life of hard manual labour, like slaves longing for cool shade, like workers waiting for their pay. Month after month I have nothing to live for; night after night brings me grief . . . My days pass by without hope, pass faster than a weaver's shuttle. Remember, O God, my life is only a breath; my happiness has already ended' (Job 7 verses 1–3, 6 and 7). If that last verse is not a description of despair, then I have no idea what is. Job did not deny God, but he *was* honest and he *was* in despair.

At the beginning of this chapter the definitions of the words 'hope' and 'despair' are given. Despair is 'to be without hope'. Well, we may be – materially, emotionally, and in other ways. Admitting this does not deny the reality of our hope in Christ, which of course is actually certainty, and not a nebulous hope which is not really quite sure!

Going back to our paradox of pain, 'life can hurt and go on hurting. Our loving God is still in control.' Well, it's kind of the same with feelings of despair – things can be 'hopeless'. We may have lost everything, but our hope can still be in God. I can hear someone say: 'Well, if that's the case, then why can't we trust God for everything?' The answer to that is that ultimately we can, but when we have been deserted by our spouse, or if the marriage has collapsed, all our certainties are wiped away in one. We may be unlucky enough to lose material things as well, like our home and/or our source of income. Life can and does feel hopeless at times like these, but our loving God is still in control.

Let me tell you what happened when I managed to stop crying in my hall that day in the vicarage. For a long time I just lay there, too exhausted to move. Life did indeed feel hopeless. I was about to lose my home and I *had* lost my husband, my role, my church, my ministry. I had lost my very identity and there were still massive problems to sort out, like trying to provide for two daughters and myself, and a hundred and one other things, but as I lay there that day I suddenly knew that Christ was lying even lower than I was on that carpet. It was the most extraordinarily powerful experience. I felt He was there with me and because I was too weak to put my hand out to Him, *He* was reaching out to me! I could almost see His hand stretched out towards me. I remember, I physically reached out to where I knew He was beside me and I just said two words: 'Help me.' When I eventually stood up, I knew again with renewed certainty that He was indeed my hope for the present and the future. But all the same problems remained. The present was still almost unbearably painful and the future just as terrifying.

Christine describes her despair in words as follows: 'The entire situation made me feel despair, but in particular the loss of all that constituted my perception of my identity. In a short space of time I lost my husband and the expectation of our continuing life together, and my house, my garden, my way of life and place in society. My son was abroad, my elder daughter emigrated, my younger daughter was at boarding school and the dog died! In addition, I moved to an area where I knew no-one. I was bereft and lonely. Despair was absolute.'

Elizabeth speaks of her desperate feelings and at the

same time talks of her faith in God. 'I feel despair when I am very tired or exhausted. I feel despair at our present financial position. I sometimes feel despair when I think about the future, so I try not to. God knows our position. I believe He will not abandon us.'

Brenda says: 'Despair came in the rejection. Someone I loved and continue to love very dearly is not even bothered about me any more. Despair came also in the giving up of a way of life which was comfortable and to some extent protected. God had been good to us as a couple, using us in His ministry. To then go on alone is a very difficult experience with which to cope.'

I remember another face of despair which I think many people will identify with. Sitting in my flat with a bottle of pills in one hand and a glass of wine in the other, I debated with myself if I had the courage to end it all. That experience may come in many different ways. I was told by a very competent counsellor that feeling like that because life is just too painful is not usually the time that people do in fact take their own lives. It is when we reach the point of rejecting the needs of our families because we feel so worthless that we think they would be better off without us. Christians *do* reach this stage. I did, and I know others who have too. In the end, for me, I thought of my daughters and I realised that it would make God grieve very much if I went through with it. He showed me that I was of worth to *Him* even though I felt utterly worthless myself. What I do not understand is why this happens to some of us and not to others. That is one of my still unanswered questions.

Recently I lost a dear Christian friend who took her own life and I do not pretend even to begin to understand it. It was about this time that I wrote the following:

Why?

Why God – why?
My soul cries out to You.
A silent scream which echoes
Round and round
– Why God – why?

The magnitude of what is happening
overwhelms me – swamps me.
And where are You God?
Where are You?
Where are Your arms of love?

No eloquent phrases come to mind –
No trite speech of acceptance.
I toss and turn in circles of bewilderment –
Pushed, pulled, sat upon –
There is no comforting place of rest.

No answers to ease the hurt –
And it is so hard to live with the questions.
I'm tired God – tired in every possible way –
Reach down my Father and hold me
– For I have no strength left to reach up to You.

There is nothing I can do – nothing – except
Live the pain, feel it, experience the hurt –
And being too weak to lift it to You –
I ask You 'Father, could You please
Reach down and hold me ever closer to Your heart?'

I went to an Anglo-Catholic conference a few weeks after my husband had left me the second time. There were many things still left unsettled and I was feeling very bad indeed. One of the two speakers that year was Bishop Lindsay Urwin, whom I greatly respected and liked. He is a superb speaker, but suddenly as he spoke he hit a nerve and I had an awful job not to start crying where I sat. Something he said released something in me and at the end of his talk I managed to stagger over to where he was standing. I looked at him and said simply: 'I'm in hell.' He didn't show any shock or disapproval. He looked back at me and said equally as simply: 'I rather thought you were.' In that simple sentence he gave me 'permission' to be in hell. He also showed me that he accepted *me* because he accepted my pain and the extent of it. Later we talked and he helped me tremendously by his understanding and his unconditional acceptance of how I said it was for me. He didn't try to contradict me or tell me how *he* thought it was for me. He stayed with me where I was and walked a little way with me. That is what Christ did for people. He met them where *they* were, not where *He* wanted them to be. By doing that, Lindsay showed me the acceptance of Christ, even though I felt I was indeed in hell.

Some Christians would be shocked just to have heard me say that, but honesty shocks a lot of people. The one Person it never shocks is our Lord. He longs for us to be honest with Him about our feelings and He longs for us to be honest with each other too.

Our pain makes us the person we are. Along with all our other human attributes, it forms our personality. If we deny our pain, then we deny ourselves. Christians who cannot cope with the pain of other Christians reject a large part of them. That brand of religion which encourages us to deny our real feelings of pain and despair is responsible for much heartache and frustration. It is looking at someone's pain, trying to ignore it, and thus ignoring them. If we don't know what to say, then best to say nothing! A hand on a shoulder, or an arm around it, is far more comforting than empty words.

After my husband left me the first time, on two separate occasions I bumped into two fellow 'clergy wives' in town who had recently been bereaved. Each one said to me before I had a chance to say anything, that what I was going through was worse than what they were suffering. They said that even though it was dreadful for them they did not have the element of rejection to cope with as well. I want to say here before I say anything else that in no way at all am I belittling the pain of bereavement. My own sister lost her husband recently and I have seen at first hand the dreadful suffering it brings. In the subtitle to this chapter I describe despair as 'A Pain Beyond Bereavement', not necessarily because it's worse but it goes beyond in that, because of the elements of rejection and betrayal, we have other things with which we have to come to terms as well as loss.

I remember at my brother-in-law's funeral, standing very close to the coffin, and being totally overwhelmed by my feelings as well as my tremendous feelings of grief for my sister, I looked at the big wooden box and suddenly found myself wishing so much that I had a 'body' to bury too. My marriage had ended but I had nothing to bury. In a very real way, there was no neat end to the death of my marriage. It is recognised in bereavement that after the funeral the next stage of grief can begin. With no burial, no funeral, I suddenly felt 'stuck' where I was, and found myself wondering how I was ever going to be able to move forward on to the next stage of my own personal journey of grief.

Those of us who have been rejected cannot bury that rejection. We have to live with it on a daily basis. It comes back at us from the most unlikely sources and we are constantly reminded of it in a hundred different ways. My sister's husband did not choose to leave her; death separated them. The death involved in desertion is the death of love, commitment and trust. How do you bury those? The effects of them leave deep scars. When we bury our spouses, we know they go saying, in effect: 'I do not want to leave you. I would stay if I could. I love you.' Knowing this helps the pain of bereavement a little. When we are deserted, our spouses go saying in actuality: 'I want to leave you. I wouldn't stay if I could. I do not love you.' The former gives comfort; the latter gives deep and lasting pain. That is why desertion is beyond bereavement.

The dictionary definition of bereavement is 'to rob of anything valued . . . to snatch away.' The definition of rejection is 'to throw away . . . to discard.' Both these things leave us feeling alone, hurt and bereft. Put all that together and it is no wonder that it leads to despair, for in some cases that which we have been robbed of is hope itself.

Brenda puts this so very well. 'I spent a whole hour weeping. I thought I could get through the whole day without crying, but no, it's worse than ever. I miss him so much. He is in everything around me, everything I do. I can't understand why he has left me. What has she got that I can't give him? How can he be committing such an awful sin, Lord? I keep crying out, but You don't seem to hear me, Lord. I rang him and he said he didn't realise it was so hard for me. He tried to cheer me up by saying that I would see him tomorrow, as though that would make up for my not having him here with me. I don't know whether seeing him makes it more difficult. I am like a girl on a date, but this lover just leaves me to be with someone else. It's tearing me apart, and I am afraid because I am finding it very easy and logical to consider suicide . . . I feel bereft and alone. That is a way out of it all. I must stand firm on my Rock and resist this. Jesus has the victory.'

Christine found that her despair quite simply led to depression, while Robert's experience was quite different from all this. Of the word despair he says: 'Despair . . .! I find that hard to understand. Again my background is of use to me. We were taught . . . 'all things come to an end one day'. That is true . . . the awful miseries of boarding school . . . eventually ended. Likewise the awful days in the army . . . did the same. Forced marches, laden with physical pain and exhaustion . . . came to an end. Life goes on; it has its own flow. You are part of it.

'What you need is endurance . . .? How long can you hang in there . . .? You deal with the present moment. Can you stand the present moment? Yes, just. Good, keep it like that – you will win through. You need endurance and patience. If you pray for it, it is amazing how far you will go and how much you will endure – far more than you would ever dream of. The survivor mentality is important.'

So what can we do at those times when despair eventually overtakes us? Well, as Christine and Robert say, we can pray – except that sometimes we can't. Sometimes prayer is just too difficult. But what do we mean by prayer? There are a hundred different answers to that! When we feel despair, the one thing we need is one little word – Jesus, that's all. I find just to whisper it is enough. We don't need long eloquent prayers. We don't need peace in our hearts. We don't need to be thinking or feeling 'the right thing' (whatever that is!). We just need, that's all. Psalm 139 verse 2 – my very favourite! – says: 'You know everything I do; from far away you understand all my thoughts.' How wonderful! So, just to whisper His name is enough – that *is* our prayer and He will honour it.

There are other things we can do, too. Sometimes our prayer, our unspoken need, is met by being given the strength – just enough strength – to actually *do* something about the way we feel. Elizabeth says: 'It's so helpful to talk to another person who has been through a similar experience. I sometimes even end up sharing laughter. I am lucky to have very good friends who have been brilliant. Their care and friendship is so important to us all. My next door neighbours have been a wonderful support and are now precious friends. That's something positive that has come out of this terrible experience. I see a Christian counsellor who has truly been sent by God. She has helped me greatly in so many ways. I have a wonderful mother – I honestly do not know how I would have coped without her care and love for us all.'

But some people do not have such a caring network of friends and family, or sometimes we feel we simply do *not* want another person near us. I think I discovered the important thing most times is to *do* something – it doesn't really matter what. It can be a walk – getting out of the house is a good idea. If it is pouring or we are shattered, playing the piano can help or if we don't do that then perhaps writing. If we don't write, then perhaps we could hit a golf ball or stamp on the floor. Sometimes I have found that if it is very bad I simply have to go to sleep. I do not think there is anything wrong with this; sleep can bring relief from the pain, and after sleep things can look a tiny bit brighter – maybe because we feel a tiny bit refreshed. I suppose the danger in that is that we can use sleep as a panacea for everything and be tempted to give up and just stay in bed, but there are definitely times when we need to 'switch off', put our heads down, pull up the duvet, and temporarily get out of the situation which is causing us such distress.

In my time I have even rung the Samaritans, before I got to know people and make friends in my new town. At the back of this book there is a list of people to contact if you feel really alone or in any kind of need. We may not care enough about ourselves to feel like ringing anyone, but the Samaritans, for example, are trained to listen to people who do not know what to say.

One very practical thing I *have* found useful – and I have heard other people say the same – is to have something to look forward to. It is not a lot of help right in the middle of an attack of the deepest despair, but it can just swing the balance. It's a hook to hang our feelings on, something to hope for which will *be* fulfilled because it is under *our* control. It does not necessarily have to be something big or expensive. If it *does* happen to be a round-the-world cruise, so much the better! No, I am talking about things like a trip to the hairdressers or the theatre. It may even be something as simple as a box of chocolates. I remember once, when I had been in great distress, I put my coat on, walked down the road to my local shop – in itself a miracle, *me* walking! – and bought myself a small box of Milk Tray. Then I sat down, selected a TV programme, poured a glass of wine, put my feet up and made serious inroads into the said box of chocolates. Believe me, it was even worth the migraine I had as a result!

Sometimes a meal with a friend is really good in the 'looking forward to' stakes or going to a film with someone else – it can be anything we like doing. For ladies, if finances allow, a new pair of shoes or new jeans can work wonders. It probably sounds really trite, but it helps, and if we work full-time we need to give ourselves some 'treats' on a regular basis as funds allow. Otherwise life becomes work, sleep, pay the bills, work, sleep, pay the bills . . . Break the monotony – go to stay with those friends who keep inviting you for a weekend. It really is incredible what a little something to look forward to can do in terms of lifting us just enough to keep despair at bay until we feel a bit better.

Sometimes, after twenty-five years of marriage, I find I miss touch very much. I do not mean here sexual contact but just another human being touching me. The therapeutic value of touch is well known now. So occasionally, when I can afford it, I book a back and neck massage. I feel for that short time pampered and as though I am honouring my body by spending money and time on it, and it *does* help a sometimes very painful back too!

A word here about doctors. I have less than no time at all for that way of thinking which considers it wrong to go to the doctor's. I wonder what those who think that would do if they had broken their leg. Would they be so keen to hobble about on it? Would they think it wrong to go to the hospital and get it plastered? I have been very fortunate in having a very good and under-standing G.P. who has realised how difficult my life has been, and often still is. There may well come a time for you when you need to go and see your doctor. There is nothing to be ashamed of in this. We are hon-ouring ourselves much more by admitting when we need medical help, than by denying it and pretending that prayer on its own is enough. Some people will be shocked by that last sentence, but it does not stop it being true. So if you are feeling at the end of your rope, take yourself off to your G.P., and if he or she really does not understand then take advice from others and find a doctor who does. I personally find it very help-ful to have a doctor who is a Christian but this does not have to be the case for everyone – nor can it be. Anti-depressants, if you need them, are not a cure – they are a prop while we get better. Sometimes our doctor may arrange for us to have counselling if he or she thinks it may help. I do not mean that everyone who feels at the end of their tether and goes to the doctor gets put on medication, but sometimes it is necessary. If we have been through a major trauma other things may be wrong. There's nothing like a good dose of stress for raising a previously normal blood pressure! And before we all start getting to be real hypochondriacs, all I am saying here is: be aware that at some stage you may need to admit you need medical help.

Despair has many faces, but so too does hope. It could be in the face of a friend. It might be in the love of a son or daughter's hug, in a phone call from a fam-ily member or a little note telling us how much some-one cares. It may be in a clear blue sky or a remembered kindness, in the soft fur of a kitten as it rubs against our legs, or in a smile or a kind word. We may feel it in a shaft of sunlight or see it in a painting, experience it as we watch ballet or play a round of golf; we may touch hope in the meeting of two minds or in a warm conversation with a friend, feel it in shared laughter. We may find it in church or we may hear it in a sermon or a song.

I want to end this chapter by relating something that happened to me not very long ago. I was feeling pretty low, having a really bad patch. I was dreadfully tired and beginning to wonder just how I could keep on going on. So one morning in my prayer time before I went to work, I said to God: 'Please, Father, show me something today to prove to me that You are in my life.' I went to work and as I remember I was pretty busy. Once or twice, I thought: 'Well, I may work in a convent, but I still haven't seen that sign I asked You for!'

I was actually driving home when it happened. It had been raining, but as I drove the rain stopped and the sun came out. Then I saw it – the most brilliant and beautiful rainbow I have ever seen – in front of me. It was so bright it had a shadow and spanned the road. I remember thinking how beautiful it was and I knew immediately that it was the sign I had asked God for. I thought that as I drove towards it, it would move and disappear, but it did not and I drove right through it and could look back on it. I knew God had sent the first rainbow as a sign that never again would He flood the earth. I knew He was sending this one to reassure me that He would never leave me and was indeed very much in my life. My heart lifted, and although all the same problems were still there, that reassurance was enough to give me the strength to go on. I knew He understood. Sometimes we feel as though He is the only One who does. That is how I felt when I wrote the following poem.

'Except God . . .'

Nobody can ever know about the pain.
They can be kind and try to understand,
They can speak to me of 'time healing',
They can tell me how well I'm doing,
They can even speak to me of God.
But however hard they try – and try they do –
They can never, never know about the pain.

An evening's fun, good company, a shared meal,
Things remembered, memories talked about,
All this is tinged – spoilt a little by the reality of now.
Looking back brings searing, unimaginable agonies
Which threaten to consume, to take control.
In a way, you want them to – it's too hard to try,
Too hard to keep the lid on, for they simply won't
stay buried.

The memories are too much to do with now.
And have I the energy left to cry?
Dare I? Dare I let go . . .?
If the tears do come, then they consume, devour,
The last shreds of dignity, the last semblance of
humanity gone.
They take all that is left of energy, then go on taking,
Until with exhaustion comes blessed oblivion and a
temporary release.

However hard they try, however kind they are,
They can never, never know about the pain.
It is frightening in its intensity, relentless in its tenacity,
But they want to tell you how well you look
– how happy,
For another's pain is so disturbing, so threatening.
And afraid of being 'a bore' – afraid of being 'miserable',
You agree, say – 'Yes, that after all time does heal.'

But nobody can ever, ever know about the pain -
Except God - my Father.

Chapter Eight

DIVORCE – THE DECREE ABSOLUTE

I stood in my flat staring at the letter in my hand. I had just come in from work and was feeling pretty tired – as usual! I was going out with my sister to the ballet in London that night, and until I opened the letter, I had been thinking about really important things, such as what to wear! As soon as I had seen the cream envelope, my heart had begun to work in fifth gear and I had felt breathless and panicky. It had been like this for just over a year now. One gets to recognise solicitors' letters with an accuracy akin to the latest radar scanning equipment!

Great chunks of the terrible black writing leapt off the page at me '. . . pleased to enclose the decree absolute. This is the document which finally brings your marriage to an end . . . you are now free to remarry if you wish to do so . . . you legal status has changed and you are now a divorced person.' These remarks were from the solicitor's letter. The actual document of the decree absolute was stunningly short. I counted the lines. Ten lines of type on a stark white sheet of paper. At least the solicitor's letter was on a softer cream page, matching the much dreaded cream envelopes.

Ten lines of print to end nearly thirty years of marriage. Nearly half a lifetime of loving and laughing together. Hoping and praying together. Rejoicing together over the birth of a baby. Sharing jokes, sharing dreams, just being together, chatting, and it should have been – *always* together.

But here was this dreadful page – the black words

danced before my eyes and almost seemed to mock me. They glared defiantly up at me: 'The Petitioner . . . The Respondent . . . it is hereby certified that the said decree was on (and then the date) made final and absolute and that the said marriage was thereby dissolved.' Some people, I know, are pleased to get their decree absolute. Where mutual love has ended it can be a release, and maybe they may want to remarry, already being in another relationship. But for the rest this piece of paper is bad enough. For Christians, it can be utterly devastating. For *anyone*, Christian or otherwise, who believes in their marriage vows, who still loves their husband or wife, the 'decree absolute' is aptly named, for there are 'absolutely' no words which can describe the feelings on receiving this marital death warrant. The room spun, I felt sick and giddy. I did what anyone who still loves does at that moment. I sat down, and wept, and wept, and wept.

In the event I think it was a very good thing that I had to go out that evening. I really do not know what I would have done otherwise. My sister and I travelled up to London and met my daughters at Charing Cross. As we walked across the station, I linked arms with my girls, and whispered that I had received the decree absolute that day. I didn't know what I expected their reaction to be, but it was certainly not what happened! My elder daughter hugged me tight and said in a loud voice: 'Congratulations!' As we walked out of the station on to the London street, she pointed both hands at me and shouted very loudly: 'Men – this way!' We all ended up laughing helplessly like schoolgirls, about four 'loose' women on the streets of London! Then we went into the nearest cocktail bar and had a *very* stiff drink!

Even in the midst of one of my blackest days, there was a lighter moment – and that laughter felt tremendously good. It really *is* an excellent medicine. It can diffuse the power in many situations. I still hurt and ached inside, but joining with the three people I love most in the world in a bout of uninhibited, and completely helpless laughter, lightened my spirit, lifted my heart, and did me far more good than anything else that night. No amount of comfort from friends or well meaning advice would have helped me half as much.

The ballet was performed by one of my favourite dance companies – the Rambert Dance Company. One of the dances was called 'Stabart Mater' – Mary at the foot of the Cross watching Jesus die. As I watched what on its own account was a very moving dance, how much I empathised with Mary. For as she watched her Son die, and moved accordingly, I moved with her and felt with her, for I knew I was watching the personification of the death of my marriage. Just as I had stood and stared at the decree absolute earlier that day, now I watched a dancer acting that out as she watched Jesus, her hopes and her dreams, die. As a liturgical dancer myself, I truly think I could have joined her every step of the way. I felt at that moment, the 'holding Grace' of God as I lived, with that dance, the death of our most precious hopes. My sister is also my closest friend, and with her and my two much loved daughters, I had laughed until I cried earlier that evening. Now I cried again, as I watched someone doing what *I* love to do most in the world – to dance. I wept as she expressed the sorrow I felt as I finally lost the man I loved so much. Small wonder I wept, but silently this time in the darkness of the theatre. But I knew God held me, and had provided that night all I needed to get up the next day and face the rest of my life – alone.

I have seen other people on the same day as they have received their decree absolute and witnessed the same shock and disbelief mirrored on their faces. I am thinking of one friend in particular, who on her own admission, no longer loved her husband. But on the day her decree absolute came through, she was completely stupefied. Maybe for us, as Christians, we really

121

do think it is something that only happens to someone else.

There are those of us – quite a few I suspect – who before our own divorces, said rather grandly: 'I don't believe in divorce.' I know I did. But faced with a persistently unfaithful husband and a life in shreds, there really was no other option. We can draw out the agony and wait five years – but then we risk the near certainty that they will then divorce us, however unwilling we are. And as the law stands at the moment, after five years, there is absolutely nothing we can do about it.

Would I describe divorce as a necessary evil? I don't really know, but I suppose that comes the nearest to what I feel about it now. It's one of those things that can be, and so often is, misused. There are those who go into marriage thinking: 'Well, if it doesn't work out, we can always get divorced.' Where there is no Christian faith, maybe that argument is a little easier to comprehend. But lots of non-Christians too, value the sanctity of marriage, so the whole thing is a 'mine field' of emotions and ideas.

No one has the right or the authority to judge for another person what they 'should' feel or think about divorce. Even our personal interpretations of the Bible differ, so quoting scripture – again, usually out of context – can be tricky here. Obviously we have to listen very carefully to what God says to us through the Bible, especially about something as important as divorce, but if we want to, we can prove almost anything by quoting verses taken completely out of their original context, and giving no credence to their historical or cultural setting. I hate 'verse slanging', and think it can actually be quite dangerous. We need to look at the context, and all sorts of things, before we can make a valued judgement on what the Bible says on any given subject. If in fact it says anything at all! There are some seemingly very important subjects that it appears to remain annoyingly silent upon! Unfortunately, those are usually the very ones *people* don't remain silent on, and thus we get all sorts of irrelevant verses thrown at us! I believe completely in the Bible as the inspired Word of God, given to His people through the power of the Holy Spirit. I also believe completely in the intelligence which God has given us to interpret that truth in a relevant way for our society today. Otherwise it loses its power. The eternal truths remain the same through all eternity, but we must seek to make those truths relevant to our culture and society, or we have nothing to offer people in the 'Godless' world of today.

For myself, I believe with all my heart in the sanctity of marriage. I believe that marriage is for life – as we say when we take our marriage vows. I believe that barring things such as mental illness, abuse, some addictions, or changes in sexuality, there is nothing that cannot be worked at and sorted out IF BOTH PARTIES ARE WILLING. And that really is what it depends on. *Both* parties being willing. And that is why adultery is such a killer, because it robs one of the people in marriage, of the willingness to work at their relationship.

Marriage is a sacrament given by God, to two people. It is not something we can glibly, or in any way, choose to walk away from. It is for life – 'for better, for worse – for richer, for poorer – till death us do part.' And that death is not referring to death of the commitment on one side of the marriage – it means actual physical death. We take our marriage vows before Almighty God, and it is a very solemn and precious moment. We make promises before Him and all our families and friends. God has promised us eternal life through His Son. What would we feel like if we got to heaven and He said: 'Oh sorry – you can't come in. I've changed my mind!'? Shocking, isn't it? I do not think I could stand before Him and say: 'Oh, my marriage? Sorry God – I changed my mind.' He'd say: 'But you promised . . .' And it's not fear of His judgment that

123

makes me say this. It's fear of His love.

Marriage is a sacrament, and it *cannot* be taken on board lightly, or dismissed because we are breaking one of God's commandments and committing adultery with someone else. I know one of the arguments used is: 'Oh well, God is a God of love, and He understands.' Yes, He does. He understands that that person has not been willing to stay faithful, and work at their marriage. He understands that they have put their own desires first, and rubbished one of His most precious gifts to us. I sometimes wonder if those talking so glibly about God's 'understanding', really understand themselves what they are talking about. And in some cases, I think it is the only way they can handle their own guilt, which they are unable or unwilling to face up to. To throw away the sacrament of marriage is to cause untold heartache and despair, and it grieves the heart of God to breaking point, and beyond.

The book of Malachi in the Old Testament, was written to recall the people and priests to renew their faithfulness and their covenant with God, but it is done through the analogy of marriage, and the principles are the same as those pertaining to a marriage covenant. In Chapter 2, verses 14b – 16, God says: '. . . She was your partner, and you have broken your promise to her. . . . Didn't God make you one body and spirit with her? What was his purpose in this? . . . So make sure that none of you breaks his promise to his wife. "I hate divorce" says the Lord God of Israel. "I hate it when one of you does such a cruel thing to his wife. Make sure that you do not break your promise to be faithful to your wife." Strong language. One of the reasons why God hates divorce so much is that He knows well the pain and heartache it causes to all concerned. It really is impossible to describe in words what it does to one to see in front of them the marital death sentence which the decree absolute is. Some of the feelings of devastation experienced can be due to the expectation that your life together will be, indeed, until death does separate you. And suddenly, that life is no more. I do not think there can be a more thorough trauma, for it involves absolutely every part of our being, body, mind, spirit, and of course heart. To have it all stripped away from one is to be robbed of the very meaning of life – or so it feels. It is intrusive in its ability to abuse all our finer feelings of security and belief in another person, and perhaps far more damaging than that, our belief in ourselves. It takes every ounce of courage and faith we possess to hang on to our integrity, and in some cases our very desire to actually stay alive. Not for nothing did the God who loves us so much, plan marriage 'till death us do part'. Even now, nearly five years later, I still feel on some days, as though I have been torn in two.

Brenda describes her feelings on receiving her decree absolute as follows: 'I felt sick. There were lots of tears.' But for her there was also a sense of relief, because recognising the death of her marriage, she had taken the step to divorce her husband. 'I felt a sense of relief at having made, and carried through, a decision.'

But I know for myself, that even having take the step to instigate an inevitable divorce, the feelings of hurt, and the trauma of it all, are none the less. We may have only taken what to us is an alien decision, to regain some control of a life which we may feel is controlled by two other people. In fact, I think it sometimes makes it worse, because we are doing something which is, in our hearts, against what we truly believe. We may well be doing it for very good reasons, but compromise is not always an easy friend.

Elizabeth believes there is a place for divorce, especially in cases of adultery.

Christine says that when she received her decree absolute, she simply felt 'numb'.

Robert's view is more liberal towards divorce. He speaks both as a priest, and as a man. 'My views on divorce are in a word, liberal. Marriages can break and die. They obviously do. At the onset everybody starts with the good intentions of making the adventure a success. This is not always guaranteed. Human beings are amazingly complex, and the world is stressful and hard. Yes, there will be failures, and success in marriage. This has to be recognised. Let's celebrate the success, and let that be everybody's aim. But let us also be caring and compassionate to those who fail the enterprise. That is Christian also. Let us be as thoughtful and compassionate as possible. It is very helpful if couples can informally, or better, formally, release one another from their marriage vows. I found that helpful to do informally.'

Obviously here, Robert is talking about couples who have mutually agreed to part. For myself, I do not think there is *any* way I could have released my husband from our marriage vows before the decree absolute took that choice away from me.

There are just so many things we lose when suddenly our spouses leave us, and so many of those things become 'officially' lost to us when we receive our decree absolute. As well as all the things people talk about like home, job, position, companionship, loss of security, there are the things people don't talk about. Well, not much in Christian circles anyway. Things like the physical side of the marriage relationship, which in a day, is gone. After sometimes many years of being married, that is a tremendous loss and bereavement, and brings many problems of its own. A large part of our self worth, self fulfilment, and self giving is tied up in it. Obviously it is one aspect of loss which, being so intimate, we are very careful in whom we confide about it. But because it is such a large part of any marriage relationship, it cannot be ignored, and the loss of it has to be addressed. Non Christians find difficulty in understanding our dilemma, because for them that dilemma does not exist! But it is real for us – it is both painful and insistent, and we have to learn to find personal coping mechanisms to deal with it. Any hard physical exercise helps. I remember when I was first on my own, the force of my feelings shook me, and I did not know quite what to do, so I wrote it all down. I called it simply 'Night'.

It's four in the morning and the pain chases sleep away.
Memories rush in, surging and wrapping
themselves around me like an angry tide,
that crashes relentlessly
stabbing and holding my heart,
till I am left breathless and reeling onthe shore.
Why hope for sleep anyway, when often it brings
only dreams of him?

And when did his love die – and why did it die?
I did not change.
What was it in me he pushed away – turned from?
And what was there in me that could not hold him
– and would not, if I could – for he does not want me.

And how do I stop the ache and the longing to feel
his arms around me?
The longing to lean against him and be held –
protected – loved?
And how do I stop wanting him?
And how do I stop remembering nights of tender,
life giving love?

Memories, relentless as the tide, crash mercilessly
over my body and my mind.
My soul screams out: 'My God, my God, why have You
forsaken me?'

And what is love anyway?
Love is selflessness – our own needs giving way to
those of the other.

And what is hope in love?
Hope is thinking that one day it may just be
possible for his love to return.

And what is joy in love?
Joy is knowing that you are loved.

I have no love from him – no hope – no joy.
What then – am I dead?

Deep, never ending sadness cries to God
'Father, forgive them, for they know not what
they do.'

An eerie silence is left.
No reason – no shape – just nothingness.

And so I wait – I wait as He did.
For the resurrection.

Several years after I wrote that 'scribbling', whilst on
my own this final time, I penned the following. I
thought long and hard about whether to include it or
not. I decided I would, as I know there will be those
who identify with it.

There is a longing
too deep, too intimate
to be spoken of.
The body yearns,
The heart craves.
The mind reaches out.
For what was –
But is no more.

A joining which gives
joy to the body,

peace to the mind.
The rites of womanhood,
which in a day –
were taken.
And my heart, and my body
– ache.

To think that now he shares
all this with another
is crucifixion –
a private, intimate agony.
Indescribable, and raw.

Lord, take my body –
take my mind –
take my heart.
But take also, my soul –
That part of me he never, never touched.
For that was ever
and will always be,
Yours and Yours alone.

It is the hardest thing in the whole wide world, I know, but the only way we can get through divorce is eventually, when we are able, to see it not only as an ending, but also as a beginning. This does not happen overnight! The shock and grief, the sense of loss, the sheer pain of it all has to be worked through, again, at *our* speed. There is no 'proper' length of time, so I shall not even suggest one. Some people take longer than others, and that's just fine. Take as long as you need – it is *your* divorce, *your* pain, *your* trauma, and *your* life. Don't let anyone make you feel guilty because you are taking longer than either them, or someone they know. We are all different, and you are unique, and God loves you just that way!

But in the end, divorce *is* a beginning. It is, because it has to be. After the grieving, to see it as such is the only way to get through. It marks a stage in our lives, which may well have been forced on us by others, but nevertheless, it *is* a stage, and one we have to move on from.

When we are ready, if we want to, we can begin dating again. This can feel very strange after such a long time, and we may well have forgotten the ground rules, but I guess it can be fun finding them out! We can join a Christian singles group, or dating agency. When we do eventually come to a point of acceptance of our divorce, it actually feels quite good to realise that we have taken control back in our lives, and now we can do as we choose, and not as someone else dictates. We are our own person now, and quite often for those of us who want it, there is someone out there waiting for us, if we are brave enough to 'push a few doors'. We may feel that we would prefer to stay single. That's absolutely fine – it's *our choice*, and that feels good.

Ideas about remarriage after divorce amongst Christians, are many and varied. And that is how it should be, because as individuals, we are many and varied, and each situation and circumstance is different. There cannot be one hard and fast rule about this. It is up to the individuals concerned to do what they feel in their heart, and work out in their minds, to be true and real for them. I know *I* have prayed and thought about this, and if the right man came along, if I felt it to be right, I would remarry. I hasten to add that I have not yet been asked! It does say, in Matthew's exception clause, in chapter 5, verse 32: 'But: I tell you now: if a man[woman] divorces his[her] wife[husband], for any cause other than her[his] unfaithfulness, then he[she] is guilty of making her[him] commit adultery if she[he] marries again.' So for myself, because my husband committed adultery, and now we are divorced, I feel it would be right for me to remarry.

Robert puts it very well: 'Remarriage. Yes, a good prospect. Depends on lots of things. Only when fruitful reflection has been done, and after much healing. Distance is important. That is, having been on their own a good length of time. If I were to stipulate I would say 'five years'. The church should not shy away from the blessing of (some) remarriages, or even of taking them. I do, and I find them to be very sincere and good occasions.'

Elizabeth believes there is also a place for remarriage, although she does not expand on this.

Brenda says: 'I have mixed feelings about remarriage. If the right person came along, was a believer, and after much heart searching and prayer, I think I would seriously consider it.'

There are stories of Christians who have remarried and are very happy. This is so for Neil and Margaret. When Neil married his first wife, they were both very young and inexperienced. After an initial year of happiness, things began to go badly wrong. The couple had children, to try and cement the relationship, but it only highlighted the fact that the marriage would not have stood on its own. As they all became more involved in the life of the church, Neil became increasingly aware of his loveless marriage, and says that because his wife did not love him, eventually she came to dislike him intensely. He became disillusioned and life lost its meaning and purpose, even though he continued to pray about the situation and sought advice. He felt that there was no mutual will to revive the love. In the end, Neil became quite suicidal. Neil prayed and asked God to give him real love. He felt that God promised him he would find it.

About six months after this, he went to a weekend conference which his wife encouraged him to go on. It was at this conference that Neil met Margaret, and he says: 'We talked and talked, as if we had known each other for years.'

On Sunday the conference ended with a Eucharist, or Communion service, and Neil knew that he had to sit with Margaret. During the service Neil heard God say to him softly and gently: 'You asked me for real love – well, here she is!'

On returning home, Neil told his wife that he now agreed to a divorce. There was a mutual understanding between them that an end had come to the intolerable conflict for them both.

Eight months after his decree absolute, Neil and Margaret were married, and as he puts it: 'We continue to share the joy I never thought possible. Day by day I learn the meaning of real love as God had promised me. My prayer is that our joy may provide an encouragement for others.'

Having seen Neil and Margaret together, I can only say that watching them certainly gives joy to me. Their love for each other is so obvious, and their happiness so tangible, that it is easy to see how God has guided them together. They are so *right* for each other, and it reminds me, every time I see them, that out of heartbreak and despair, true happiness can, and does, grow. I wish them continued joy, and thank God for them.

Divorce has been about for thousands of years. It is mentioned in the Old Testament, and has been a part of society and different cultures all over the world. It happens to Christians and non-Christians alike. Quite often Christians will condemn other Christians because they are divorced, even though they may not know the stories of heartache and despair behind the facts. It is so easy to judge others when we are not in that position ourselves, and as with everything in life, we need to remember that: 'There but for the grace of God go I.' It is not ours either to judge, or condemn. But it is most definitely ours to be compassionate and caring to those who have suffered the undeniable trauma of divorce, which for those with a Christian faith, is enormous.

Divorce, in nine cases out of ten, brings heartache, grief and pain of many sorts. For Christians it can also bring guilt and great struggles with our faith. But the thing we need so much to get hold of is DIVORCE IS NOT A SIN. It is tragic, yes. Devastating, yes. Deeply wounding, yes. But it is *not* a sin. It is not listed in the ten commandments as one of the 'shalt nots'. Adultery is, but divorce is not.

It is a wonderful inescapable fact that we have a heavenly Father who is infinite in His understanding, and whose love is never ending. He understands all our pains and struggles with divorce. *He* does not condemn – He holds. He does not criticise – He affirms. He does not shun – He hugs. What a good thing it is, in this minefield of such different ideas about an enormous subject, that the people best qualified to speak on divorce – those of us who have been through it – can know with all certainty, above everything else, that God understands. We can know that He loves us the more because of what we have been through.

Divorce

Sometimes I still think of him.
I try not to, but after being married for so long,
it's impossible not to.
I think if him coming home from work –
but to another home, not ours.
I think about him talking about his day –
but to another listener, not me.
I think of him relaxing while his dinner is cooked
– but by other hands, not mine.
I think of him being embraced in longing –
but by other arms, not mine.
I think of him lying in bed –
but beside another woman, not me.
Memories, longing, a love abused – uselessness
and rejection.
It hurts, Father – it hurts, it hurts, it hurts.
And when the law of the land tears us apart in
divorce,

It's too enormous – too huge an agony.
Why, Father – why, why, why?
Where are You? Please, please give me an answer.

Silence . . . then, tenderly, with infinite gentleness,
'My child, I see them too – as I see you.
My grief for you all is enormous, huge.
I have only one answer my beloved one.
One answer, given in so many different ways.
I love you – I love you – I love you.
I cannot stop the memories – but I can go back
with you and relive them beside you.
I cannot stop the longing – but I can meet it with
my love.
I could not stop your love being abused – but I
held you all the time.
I will use you – to me, you have a worth beyond
price.
And I will never, never reject you.

'Daughter, the "why" you may never know, but I
am in the pain.
I am here, and my answer is love.
I think of you all the time my child, all the time.
I too hate divorce, but trust me my child, trust
me.
For I am with you always – and my answer is love.'

Chapter Nine

OTHER PEOPLE'S STORIES

Always There
Tears are
    Only a memory away
    Only a look
    Only a spoken word
    One job too much
    One extra bill
    One awkward adolescent.

Tears are only a moment's longing away
Always ready – always there.

Christ is
    Only a breath away
    Only a sigh
    Only a whispered word
    One heartbeat
    One death
    One life

Christ is only a moment's surrender away
Always ready – always there.

The next four chapters are the stories of four friends of mine, who have very courageously told of the breakdown of their marriages in the hope that it may help someone else in a similar situation.

All the stories take the form of interviews.

Brenda

Brenda is a successful businesswoman, whose husband, Jim, was a reader in the Church of England. After an affair with a woman in the congregation, Jim left Brenda, and went to live with 'the other woman'. I am grateful for, and admire, her honesty, in the way she talked to me.

Sue: 'Brenda, could you tell me when you first noticed that something was wrong with your marriage?'

Brenda: 'Well, it was possibly only a few weeks before Jim told me of his love for somebody else. It was nothing very definite, just the fact that he seemed to be distant, and also when we were on holiday a week or two before he left, he seemed to be finding fault with me for the smallest of reasons. Also when we were going for a walk, and I was really trying to be quite affectionate, he didn't want me to be affectionate at all. So there was nothing really very specific that I could point to and say was definitely a difference, apart from those things. The only other thing that I was aware of was that when I went to the prayer group at our local church, people were talking to me about the fact that there was some gossip in the village, and I was actually praying against the gossip, rather than listening to what the gossip was, and maybe in retrospect I think I should have been listening to what was being said.'

Sue: 'So, do you think they were trying to tell you about your husband?'

Brenda: 'I don't know if they were trying to tell me . . . maybe . . . yes, perhaps they were, but they weren't coming out with it fully. They were just saying that there was gossip in the village.'

Sue: 'Did you not listen because you were afraid of what it might be, or because you didn't want to gossip?'

Brenda: 'I didn't want to be listening to gossip, but I

think also, I didn't want to hear what was being said.'

Sue: 'So did it come as a complete bolt out of the blue when your husband told you he had fallen in love with someone else?'

Brenda: 'It did really. The only time I actually spoke to him about it was two or three weeks before, when he seemed to be going to Tina's and David's for any sort of piffling excuse. Then I said "Are you having an affair with Tina or something?" and he denied it and said "No, of course I'm not, don't be stupid." But he obviously was.'

Sue: 'So when he told you, what did you do?'

Brenda: 'Well, it was a Wednesday evening. It was the prayer group at our church and we usually went together. There was a phone call about half an hour before we were due to go. It was one of Jim's relatives to tell him that his aunt had died. It seemed a bit funny really, 'cos he wasn't particularly upset when his parents died – or he didn't appear to be – but he seemed to be overly upset about his aunt. I comforted him and then I said "Well, do you want to go to Bible study?", and he said no. I said to him "I'll go, and pray about it while I'm there." I went to the Bible study and about half an hour into it, I realised I needed to be at home with him. So I went home, but he wasn't there. I realised then where he'd gone, and I sat in the conservatory and read my Bible, and was crying when he came back in at about nine-thirty – that was the time I would normally be home. I said "Where have you been? Been to Tina's?" And he said "Yes, I've fallen in love with Tina and I want to go and live with her." I was just devastated, and I lay in a corner in the foetal position, and just cried. I couldn't come to terms with the fact that he wanted to go and live with a woman whose husband was still alive and in a wheelchair.'

Sue: 'What happened after that?'

Brenda: 'He stayed with me that night. He wanted to
go and sleep in the spare room, and I said "Don't
leave me. Stay in our bed." Well, of course neither of
us slept at all. I kept wanting to talk, and he didn't
want to talk – there were lots of recriminations and
I was quoting pieces of Scripture, and, of course, I
was bringing up David and Bathsheba and that sort
of thing, it was just a nightmare really that night.
The next morning he said he was going – he col-
lected a few clothes and he went. I was in the middle of looking after the bookstand at the Rank
Christian Centre at the Royal Show at Stoneleigh
which was a four-day commitment and this was
Thursday, which was the third day, and he'd
promised to help me on the Friday, so he said he
would come back on the Friday and go with me to
help me with the bookstall.'

Sue: 'That must have been very hard.'

Brenda: 'It was hard. We did it together for a bit, and
then I said to him would he look after it while I went
off at lunchtime. And I went away to talk to my
vicar and his wife, and tell them what had happened. Whilst they were shocked, they didn't seem
to be overly amazed about it. They were very
shocked that he had actually done it, but I think they
had had their suspicions.'

Sue: 'Did you feel at this time that you were very angry
with your husband and angry with God, and maybe
angry with yourself?'

Brenda: 'I don't think I was really aware at that very
early time of any emotions except complete devastation and the fact that I couldn't stop crying.
Although I'd got to look after the bookstall, and that
meant I had to be sort of aware of what was going
on, and able to carry on with the job, every time I
took a break I just walked about crying – in tears the
whole time, and that went on for quite a long period
of time.'

Sue: 'Do you mean days?'

Brenda: 'Oh yes – weeks.'

Sue: 'Do you feel that the crying actually helped you?'

Brenda: 'I didn't see it helping me at the time, but I think it probably did.'

Sue: 'I ask that because a lot of people find they can't cry.'

Brenda: 'Yes I know what you mean, but as far as being angry is concerned, I really didn't feel anger until later. I was very conscious of the fact that I needed to be making sure there was no bitterness. I didn't want that to come in at all and I felt that if I was angry that would create bitterness. I don't think I was trying to push the anger down. I think in those early days you're just numb. There must have been emotion going on, but I wasn't feeling any. I found it difficult to pray in the normal way that I pray, but I didn't find it difficult to call out to God – just to cry out and say "Jesus" and use the Jesus prayer. "Lord Jesus Christ, Son of God, have mercy on me, a sinner." I used this prayer when I was driving – when I was sitting at home, alone – when I was with other people even, and I would just keep saying it, over and over and over.'

Sue: 'Did you have a sense that God was holding you in any special way, or did you feel Him clearly at all?'

Brenda: 'Not really. I felt very far away from God. And I didn't want to be far away from God. I wanted to be close by Him, because I knew that if I could stay close He would protect me and look after me, but I couldn't really feel Him.'

Sue: 'How did you feel towards the other woman at this stage?'

Brenda: 'I couldn't believe it because she was part of our fellowship. She wasn't a lady I particularly liked. I tried to love her because she was a member of our church, but I suppose really I thought there must have been something about her that pushed me away. She did push people away because often we would try to help her in doing the work she needed to do with a fully disabled husband. She always seemed to want to do it herself and would stop us all from helping, and you couldn't get close to her at all. I think I felt that she maybe manipulated the whole situation, because she'd fallen for my husband, but also she and her husband were in debt to a lot of money, and Jim would appear to be an escape from all of that, because he had money and a car. So really it was almost like Christmas for them. He was there with his car to take them both out not only her, but *both* of them.

One of the things that I found difficult to cope with was the fact that he was prepared to go and live with her and her husband, and the husband accepted the fact that he was there.'

Sue: 'Is it still the same?'

Brenda: 'No, the husband died.'

Sue: 'It's all a rather unusual situation.'

Brenda: 'Yes. Now I can see that he accepted it, because if Jim was there it was a better life for him as well as for her. Because there wasn't any sexual relationship between him and his wife since he had a stroke eleven years previously. He was in a wheel chair and not able to talk very well. And suddenly, there was this man who would satisfy his wife and keep her happy, and also be able to bring the better things in life for him.'

Sue: 'A very unusual eternal triangle really, wasn't it? Did you feel any sort of murderous thoughts towards the other woman?'

Brenda: 'Well, yes, I have done. I can't recall whether I did in the early days, I should think I probably did. Would you actually classify this as anger? I'm saying that I wasn't angry, but maybe that *was* being angry.'

Sue: 'I would think it was.'

Brenda: 'Yes, but I think those feelings became stronger later. They were not strong at the beginning.'

Sue: 'Do you feel that was because after you'd suffered and been on your own, you realised how hard it was?'

Brenda: 'Yes, I'm sure that's right.'

Sue: 'How do you feel towards them today? How many years is it now?'

Brenda: 'Nearly four years.'

Sue: 'Do you still find it difficult to accept or to come to terms with the situation?'

Brenda: 'Yes, I do still find it as difficult and I don't actually see that altering at all. It becomes less painful because I'm becoming stronger and able to cope with the pain, but no, I'm still absolutely devastated, and times of complete devastation still affect me at the most unusual moments. I could perhaps be in the middle of Sainsburys, or walking along the street or whatever, and suddenly there's something that clicks in your mind and it all just comes pouring back in.'

Sue: 'Would you say – and I'm asking you to generalise – that you found your church, your group of Christian friends, on the whole to be understanding, or was there any of this "There, there dear, it's all right"?'

Brenda: 'My really close prayer partners were understanding beyond anything I could have thought that humanly they would be. They were an amazing support. Any time, day or night, that I needed them they would be there or I could go to them, even to staying with people overnight when I was going through really bad times – coming with me to the doctor's – just being there, inviting me for meals. I didn't eat an evening dinner in my own house for six months because there was somebody always

141

asking me to go for a meal, and that was really quite amazing.

There were some people who thought, yes, pat you on the head, you look all right, you've put your make-up on, you've read the lesson in church, so everything must be all right now. One of the things that really hit me hard, was that this had happened on July 7th, and on August 1st I had a new car which had been on order for about six months, and somebody came to me in church and said: "Oh well, you'll be all right now because you've got your new car!" '

Sue: 'Did you feel when people treated you like that, that they were actually threatened by your pain and your honesty?'

Brenda: 'Yes. They were threatened by the pain and they were afraid, and I couldn't think why they should be. I felt they were afraid of me, but it wasn't me they were afraid of, it was the pain I was in, and the way that if they had any contact with me they would in some peculiar way catch that fear and pain.'

Sue: 'They were afraid it might happen to them.'

Brenda: 'Yes. And that happened, not only in my church, it also happened in my family. My brother was not prepared to really have anything to do with me, because I'm sure that he felt fearful that if he was in touch with me the same thing could happen to him.'

Sue: 'And when they isolated you in that way, as people do – how did that make you feel?'

Brenda: 'Well, you're already feeling absolutely isolated. And then for them to do that, just seems to be piling on more rejection.'

Sue: 'And guilt?'

Brenda: 'No, I don't think I felt guilty – not at that time anyway. I don't think I ever felt an awful lot of guilt. I think I felt guilty inasmuch as there was a possibil-

ity that I hadn't done everything I could do in the
marriage, but I don't think I felt any guilt as far as
other people were concerned.'

Sue: 'No, it's false guilt if you feel that. That's why I
asked. Looking back at this distance now, what
would you say is perhaps the biggest lesson you've
learned from it all, and the biggest strength you've
gained? A difficult question, that!'

Brenda: 'Well yes, it is a difficult question, but I'm
really very clear in my mind about what it's taught
me, and that is compassion. Before all this happened
I was a successful person. I had everything I needed
in my life, including the love of Jesus and my awareness of that. Everything was going well, and I
always felt that people who were not successful,
well, to some extent, it was their own fault. I come
from an ordinary working class family. My Dad had
problems making ends meet to feed and clothe us
and I felt I'd pulled myself up by my bootstraps
from that sort of situation and become successful,
and I felt that something was lacking in people that
they couldn't do the same thing.'

Sue: 'Because you'd done it?'

Brenda: 'Because I'd done it. But what this has taught
me is that that is not the case at all. It's people's
circumstances and the situations that they find
themselves in that put them where they are today,
and we need to be compassionate with people who
are not successful and people who are poor and
needy, or homeless. I'd even go so far as to say I
have compassion for people who do awful things. I
find it in my heart to pray for someone who has
committed a really dreadful crime, for I realise that
any of us could have been in the same situation. I
can feel close to those people, because probably they
have been rejected, and everything they've tried to
do, for whatever motives, has failed.'

Sue: 'How would you say it has affected your

Christian faith?'

Brenda: 'It's grown very much stronger. I'm not sure I know any more of the mystery than I did before, but I do know that the Lord is with us all the time, that He doesn't move away. He doesn't turn His back on us. He stays with us in spite of everything that we do, and that He's just so excited when we turn back again to Him, and He opens His arms and says "Come on" – and that's it.

But it's also given me a new outlook on the whole of my life really. It's sorted out all my priorities. It isn't important that I have a beautiful home or good clothes, or all the things I liked before. I've always hung lightly on to those things. I've never had the problem that if something gets broken, it's a big tragedy – it isn't to me, because it's just an item, it's just a material possession. But I would say that even more so now, things hang lightly, and if God were to say to me "I need you to give it up because somebody else needs it" or whatever, I wouldn't find it the problem I would have found it five years ago.'

Sue: 'If you had one thing to say to somebody who found themselves in a similar situation – they've just been betrayed and are struggling to come to terms with it – would you be able to isolate one thing you would want them to hang on to?'

Brenda: 'It sounds a "pat" answer, but yes, if they could just hang on to the love of Jesus. That's it really. It isn't easy for us to do that. It sounds easy when we say it, but it isn't easy to do, because we feel betrayed even by God, don't we?'

Sue: 'Yes, well that's the problem . . .'

Brenda: 'Sometimes we actually lose God somewhere along the line. I said I didn't feel I'd been angry. But I think looking back at those very early days, I was angry sometimes, because I can recall going into the garden and kicking the tree, and I'm sure that was anger and my way of getting rid of it. But two years into this situation, I'd been away with Jennifer Rees Larcombe for a holiday, and I'd been really lifted up because she's asked me to help with her ministry. I'd come home really buoyed up with this. And then on the Thursday after returning on the Saturday, Jim rang me to ask me if the decree absolute was coming through. I asked him "Why, what's the hurry?" and he said "I want to get married on Saturday", and I just hit the bottom again and went right back down. That night I went to bed and I couldn't sleep. About one-thirty I got up and went into the conservatory, and really was very angry with God. I was reading some Psalms, and I realised there was no problem with that because David had been angry with God. This went on for about an hour, where I just shouted, and yet I was aware that God's presence was very much with me as I was being angry. In the end I cried out to Him, and said "Give me something – give me something to make me aware of Your presence with me – to make me realise that You're there. Please give me something."

And God is just amazing, because I opened my Bible, which is something I do quite frequently when I'm looking for a word, not with a preconceived idea of any verse, or with any passage in mind. I just opened it and the top left hand corner of my page that I looked at was Isaiah 54, starting at verse 5. In the NIV it says "The Lord your Maker is your husband." I'm reading now from The Good News Bible. "Your Creator will be like a husband to you – the LORD Almighty is his name. The holy God of Israel will save you – he is the ruler of all the world. Israel, you are like a young wife, deserted by her husband and deeply distressed. But the LORD calls you back to him and says 'For one brief moment I left you; with deep love I will take you back. I turned away angry for only a moment, but I ill show you my love for ever', so says the LORD who saves you."

Then I just couldn't cope with it; I was absolutely – not devastated, but broken up because God had answered my prayer so clearly, and it just reassured me that He was in it with me. He was in the whole thing with me, right from the very first day, at the centre of it, and really over the last two years I've moved forward and God's been with me – even in the bad times, and I've no doubt about it, simply from that passage. When I cried out to Him, He answered my need.'

Chapter Ten

OTHER PEOPLE'S STORIES II

Christine

Christine was married for ten years to a draughtsman who left her because he felt unable to cope with married life. They have one daughter. Christine had been married and divorced before this, and has one older child from her first marriage.

Sue: 'Christine, can you tell me when you first felt something was wrong with your marriage – when you had the feeling that everything wasn't quite as it should be?'

Christine: 'Soon after we were married but it's difficult to pinpoint. Well, things were always difficult, but I suppose I closed my eyes to them. I knew he was a difficult man, and I knew he had changed his mind about being married, that he would rather have been a bachelor. He decided this at the very beginning, and he tells me that the whole of the marriage he tried very hard to make it work, so there was always this kind of tension.'

Sue: 'Do you think that's what all the hostility was about?'

Christine: 'Yes, because his nature is that he will go all out to do something and he'd be obsessive about it, and once he's achieved it he thinks "Oh goodness, I've made a mistake, and now I realise that marrying me was in the same category." '

Sue: 'How did it come about that you separated?'

Christine: 'Well, I used to foster difficult children, had a toddler, one teenager and a baby who died at three months old. All this was going on, and I had a huge house to care for, and my health broke down. I said I realised that in order to get well, I had to shed some of the stress, and my first step would be to stop fostering. His reply was that well, if that was the case, he was going to leave me. It was about three or four years after that that he did. He just said one day "I'm going."'

Sue: 'So was that an excuse – that you weren't doing what he wanted?'

Christine: 'Yes. He saw having a wife as being a help-mate in the sense that he is very charitably minded, always has been, and one of the roles that his wife should perform was to help him with his charitable work. Hence all the people that I looked after, and if I was thinking of stopping doing that then he didn't want to be with me. I think that's really how he saw my sole work, because people would say to him "Oh you know, you're so wonderful, you look after all those people". But it was years before I realised "Wait a minute – he's at the office all day. It's *me* that's looking after all these people", and because I had them living in my house, and because they were all so emotionally needy, I was totally drained. I think one gets on to that sort of treadmill if you like, life is very busy and you just keep going, and it's very difficult to step back and see that. It's only with hindsight that I see it now.'

Sue: 'So when you married him did you love him?'

Christine: 'Yes, and I still love him now.'

Sue: 'Do you think he loved you, or do you think he was marrying you because he thought that you would help him as you've described?'

Christine: 'He claims that he's never loved anyone. He claims he's incapable of love.'

Sue: 'What about himself?'

Christine: 'Do you mean does he love himself? No, he finds that concept very difficult even as a Christian. Loving yourself is not on. And also he finds it very difficult to acknowledge the concept of a loving God. To him God is a punitive God. Love just does not figure in his emotions and he's aware of this, but when I talk to him he says "Well I hear what you say about love, but I can't feel it. I don't know what it means."'

Sue: 'Do you wonder why he felt so much compassion for those other people that you looked after?'

Christine: 'Well yes, we talked about this, and I put my theories to him about it. He says what he can't do is to keep a sustained relationship with the people that he looks after. He can go out for an hour or two a day looking after people who are very needy, and then leave them. He can't be in a relationship with his wife or children where he needs to be continuously committed.'

Sue: 'So why did he do this? Does he think he's doing it because it's a good thing to do?'

Christine: 'No, I am certain that he is a very good man and a very honourable man, and I believe him when he says he feels incredibly guilty about his actions. I think that he feels he should give to others, so he gives in the way that he knows he can, which I suppose for him at least redeems him a little in his own eyes.'

Sue: 'Has he gone into another relationship?'

Christine: 'Yes, he's living with a woman.'

Sue: 'That must have been particularly difficult for you.'

Christine: 'Yes, it was. In fact, that's what caused my depression, because for two years we were still friends, but living under separate roofs, and I could have accepted that for the rest of my life. But then he moved in with this other woman and I just fell to pieces.'

Sue: 'I'm not surprised. He rejected you by starting a relationship with someone else.'

Christine: 'Exactly.'

Sue: 'But now he wants to come back to you, which must be really hard for you?'

Christine: 'Yes, it is. My feeling now – all through it really – has been just an ineffable sadness, because I do believe he's a good man, but there's something in him that causes him to act in a self-destructive way.'

Sue: 'Did he recognise that he had problems like this – did he ever consider taking counselling?'

Christine: 'He's had lots of counselling, and this is why he married late. But he found it very lonely on his own, particularly doing the church work that he did. I find it incredibly sad, which is why I love him. I love his essence, the person I think that was meant to be.'

Sue: 'The person that's in there somewhere?'

Christine: 'Exactly, but he's been overlaid by life events and genetics . . . but the person that I can sort of touch, if you like, is a wonderful person -- which is why I still love him. Although I was so upset and traumatised by it all, I don't think that he has a malicious bone in his body. I mean, he kind of hurts people by default. I don't think he ever means to, I really don't. Our daughter thinks the same thing. I mean, we talk it over and she says: "Oh Dad drives me crazy", and then she'll say, "but I don't think he means to."'

Sue: 'So has he kept a loving relationship with his daughter?'

Christine: 'Well, as much as he can, yes. I mean, I think it says something for him that she and my older child think so much of him.'

Sue: 'That does speak highly of him.'

Christine: 'Yes, and the fact that I still love him speaks well of him. But I think he is a very tormented soul.

I really feel for him.'

Sue: 'So when you realised that you were suffering from depression – did that happen when you found out he was having a relationship with another person, or was it just a natural progression after all you went through?'

Christine: 'No, because as I said, the first two years were fine. I still lived in the matrimonial home and I was still near my friends. Life went on much the same as far as I was concerned. But then I decided that I really needed to move out of the area because he had such a high profile. Everything I did was reported back to him and I realised that I would never be able to make a life of my own. So I moved up to the Midlands, and within a very short space of time I had so much loss, and that's where I took a nosedive. My identity had always been that of wife and mother, I'd never had a career, and suddenly I found myself with no role like that, no-one to look after, and no home to look after because I rented for a while. My son was in Australia, my daughter was boarding. Even the dog died, and I was living in a place where no-one knew me. I'd go for days without talking to a soul. I had no telephone, and I nearly went over the edge, I really did.'

Sue: 'You were totally isolated.'

Christine: 'Absolutely. And I had nothing that was me, as I knew me then, in terms of my identity, that I could hang on to. It was like being cast adrift on the ocean.'

Sue: 'Asking, "who am I?" '

Christine: 'Exactly. Yes, I had a complete identity crisis. For about six months I just wanted to die. I hoped I would. I would never have done anything definite to bring it about, but every night I just hoped I would not wake up the next day.'

Sue: 'You weren't working at this time, so how did you begin to get out of it? How long did it last?'

Christine: 'Well, in my notes that I wrote at the time
... I remember I said it took about ten years before
I felt as though I had blood in my veins.'

Sue: 'So what did you do in those ten years?'

Christine: 'Existed.'

Sue: 'Just existed on your own?'

Christine: 'I wasn't interested in anything. I became a
virtual recluse.'

Sue: 'Did you have *any* friends up there or around
you?'

Christine: 'No. I started to. I only stayed up there two
years, because I realised I'd gone to a small village
and breaking into society was impossible. I did try
so hard, I helped with everything that was going –
church bazaars, you know, all the charitable things,
but no-one ever asked me out and if I asked them, it
was not returned. And then one Easter I came back
down here, and I stayed with Pat, a close friend of
mine, and her warmth and love just made me realise
that I should come back. So I did. But I had achieved
what I wanted to, which was to separate myself. I
came back as myself, not as my husband's wife.'

Sue: 'And when you came back down this way, and
saw your old friends – did that help?'

Christine: 'Well, when I came back I immediately went
on an Access course – you know, I'd only moved in
about a week and I was very aware at the time that
it was actually a deliberate survival course.'

Sue: 'Can you explain what Access means?'

Christine: 'Yes, it's access to university. You do the
equivalent of three A-levels in one year, which is
quite something from a standing start after many
years near brain death! But I knew that I had to do
something in order to keep living. I was very aware
of that. But when I did that and went to university I
didn't have time to make any friends, and my
youngest daughter went to school several miles
away, and I took her by car. So she didn't make

152

friends either, so I was quite isolated in that way too. We didn't settle, and I could never see a life for myself where we were living, but I stayed there until my daughter finished school.'

Sue: 'Do you feel more of a "whole" person now?'

Christine: 'Yes, I do. In fact it's very interesting. I lived in my last house for seven years and I could never see a life for myself. I could never project and think "Oh yes, that's a possibility" – there was always a dead end. I couldn't see anything, and as soon as I moved to the place I am now, before I joined anything or got to know anyone, I could see a life. It was quite extraordinary. I knew that there I could make a life and I have done.'

Sue: 'Do you still see your husband?'

Christine: 'Yes, sometimes. We have to, because I'm still linked to him financially.'

Sue: 'And how is that now?'

Christine: 'Well, it's OK for *me*, but for about three years he's been wanting to come back to me, so he finds it difficult.'

Sue: 'Has he ever said to you, "Christine, I think I made a horrendous mistake. As much as I can I love you." Does he ever say that?'

Christine: 'Yes. But it's just expediency. But I still feel married to him and he still feels married to me.'

Sue: 'Did you actually get divorced?'

Christine: 'Yes. *I* filed for divorce, but only after he took up with the other woman. If he'd not done that I would never have divorced him.'

Sue: 'Why was that?'

Christine: 'Because I really didn't want to.'

Sue: 'What do you feel having done that? Do you feel in any way that it helps you to move forward?'

Christine: 'No. And I still refer to him as my husband. I have to make a conscious effort to call him my former husband, and he refers to me as his wife.'

Sue: 'What would you say was your biggest regret

about it all?'

Christine: 'I remember saying to him once when we'd being praying together "You know, you and I could be a fortress," and I think that's my regret because we had the ability. We could have been quite a force and done a lot of good and I think if we'd led a Christian marriage it would have been wonderful.'

Sue: 'At the end of the day it takes two of you to be that committed.'

Christine: 'Yes, I know . . . I think another regret is that we had our baby that died. At the time I found it a very positive experience – it's what led me to doing a lot of research on death. I feel very strongly about it, and the concept of a positive death, but at the time of the divorce, I thought "What was it all about?". If we had stayed within the marriage and become stronger because of that, I could understand, but as it is it just seems another hurt, and for what reason? Part of me knows that that's not a reasonable thing to say, because when people said to me at the time "Don't you ever ask 'Why me?"' I would say "No – why not me? Babies are born with that condition, it's a fact of life – why should it not be me?" And that's the way I do look at it on an intellectual level, but on the level of the heart I feel such anguish because I think "Why? What was the point?"'

Sue: 'So looking at your life today, how would you say that the whole thing affected your faith?'

Christine: 'Well I have no faith now. I say that because as I'm sitting here, I would say "no faith", but I'm very aware that it's waiting in the wings, and I'm very aware of that, it's only a question of time, I know. But I think it's probably true that if a person is depressed, just as they have a glass wall around them and can't reach out to other people, I think so they can't reach out to God either.'

Sue: 'So when you felt you couldn't reach out to God,

did you try?'

Christine: 'Yes. I prayed, but again I felt as though there was a glass ceiling and I just felt that I wasn't reaching God at all, and as years of this went by, I stopped.'

Sue: 'You obviously felt that this was a two-way glass and He wasn't reaching you either.'

Christine: 'Well, when I was depressed I don't think I had any coherent thoughts, but now I would say no, I'm quite sure He *was* there, but I didn't have the comfort and guidance I suppose, that I sought. I didn't even have the knowledge that He was hearing my cries, because there was just nothing, it was like it had bounced back on me. This is why I say that I know God is there and I know He's waiting for me to come back. But at the time, nothing at all and really no human comfort either. When you're badly depressed, no-one can reach you. Of course, also, I was living away from people who knew my situation. If you're really depressed, it needs other people to reach in to you. You're incapable of reaching out to others. So if someone doesn't know you're in that state they don't reach in.'

Sue: 'So your isolation was really complete, wasn't it?'

Christine: 'Yes.'

Sue: 'Whilst it was understandable why you moved away, in one way it was the worst thing you could have done, because you were making yourself completely isolated.'

Christine: 'Absolutely. In restrospect it was. Having said that, I am quite sure now that I'm coming to life again. I can see that all those years of living with my own thoughts have been useful and actually getting through it and not going under completely.'

Sue: 'Do you feel it's made you a stronger person?'

Christine: 'Absolutely. Yes, I'm quite sure it has, and made me more understanding of other people. I think it's made me more in touch with life in general than I was before, and the only sadness connected with it is that I think my young daughter suffered . . . because I told you we talked, and I told her for the first time about my depression because she didn't realise it. I don't think you can be *that* depressed and the people around you aren't affected – particularly if it's a child. They don't understand what's going on and it's impossible to say. All they know is that Mummy's strange or not there or whatever it might be.'

Sue: 'But your relationship with her seems to be very good?'

Christine: 'Yes, it is. Very good. We talked about the pent-up anger and we explored that a bit. I think we've moved a step nearer.'

Sue: 'So you've obviously talked about the whole thing with your children, which is good because they have their own grief process, don't they?'

Christine: 'Oh yes. And the youngest is very philo-sophical about it. She'll say, "Well, Dad's like this and like that," and she doesn't expect anything from him. But then when I was with her yesterday, it all came out that she felt he'd let her down on many occasions. At least she's talking about it, which is good.'

Sue: 'But she knows how much you love her, which is really good.'

Christine: 'But they need a father, don't they?'

Sue: 'They *do* need a father, but children really are amazing. I mean, they're not as resilient as they make out, but life does go on and they have the most amazing way of adapting, which doesn't lessen their suffering, but I do find myself it certainly helps to lessen our anxiety about them a little.'

Christine: 'Yes, I suppose in some ways it's been help-ful for my daughter, because she's heard me moan about her father and yet always finish that with "But I still love him." And so I think she's been enabled to see that it's possible to see the faults in someone, or really get angry with them and yet still love them.'

Sue: 'You're giving her permission to see what's wrong, but to go on loving.'

Christine: 'Yes, that's right – exactly that.'

Chapter Eleven

OTHER PEOPLE'S STORIES III

Elizabeth

Elizabeth is a young mother with three small children. She is on income support. Her husband left her whilst having an affair with another woman – unlike Elizabeth, he would not describe himself as a Christian.

Sue: 'Elizabeth, can you tell me when you first felt something was wrong with your marriage, or felt things weren't quite as they should be?'

Elizabeth: 'I think I was so busy with the two small children, and being pregnant again . . . I suppose I was really tied up with that . . . there was an awful lot going on . . . I know I felt that Rick was not particularly interested in the children or myself. He did seem very distant. He didn't look at me when he spoke – he got very impatient with the children when he was at home. This became more and more noticeable throughout my pregnancy.'

Sue: 'So did you come to any conclusions as to what was the matter?'

Elizabeth: 'I know I felt terribly vulnerable myself and really tired most of the time, and guilty for feeling that way. I kept thinking things would get better – I was so busy I kept sweeping things under the carpet . . .'

Sue: 'So you had two small children, another one on the way, a house to cope with, and occasionally did supply teaching – did you feel guilty and maybe take the blame because you were so busy and tired?'

Elizabeth: 'Yes, I did. When I look back I know that he wasn't being reasonable. *I* felt I was being unreasonable by being so tired and not giving him enough time. There was always a reason. It was easier to think that it was something to do with me – then I could put it right.'

Sue: 'Yes, rather than something he'd done.'

Elizabeth: 'Yes, except that I knew I was terribly unhappy with him – with the way he treated the children and myself. He used to get so cross with them – especially the elder one. He hardly ever showed any interest.'

Sue: 'Did you ever think "I wonder if he's having an affair?" '

Elizabeth: 'Oh yes, yes I did. And I actually asked him and he said to me, "I cannot understand any man who can do that to his wife and children." '

Sue: 'He said that to you?!'

Elizabeth: 'Yes, he said that to me.'

Sue: 'And yet . . .'

Elizabeth: 'And yet he *was* having an affair. And he was having an affair before I became pregnant with my last child. And he said "It would be nice to have a third baby." '

Sue: 'So at what stage did you actually find out he was having an affair?'

Elizabeth: 'Well, things just deteriorated between us, during the pregnancy. And then when our daughter was born, I can remember in the labour ward feeling terribly vulnerable and alone, and actually frightened that he was in the same room, because it was almost as if there was somebody there who wasn't . . . caring.'

Sue: 'You felt he was detached . . .?'

Elizabeth: 'Absolutely . . . and perhaps even more than detached. Really resentful. I can remember thinking

159

"he never holds the baby", he never had his photograph taken with her until *I* said "Hold the baby, and I'll take a photo." He was out late at night, no interest, no care of me. I had a really bad womb infection soon after she was born, and I had mastitis, and I felt so ill. There was no real support from him, or any real sign he cared. I was so obviously an inconvenience.'

Sue: 'So how long after your daughter was born did you find out about this affair?'

Elizabeth: 'She was nearly four months old. I had asked him a few times – and I'd always apologised, because I felt guilty . . . it was a terrible thing to think this of my husband who was saying "No". He used to say to me he was selfish and he would change, and he wanted our family, and I actually said to him "Well, you're working really late at night" . . . the company used to pay for him to be put up – or so I thought – in a hotel. I thought he was just very tired from work. But he said he wanted to come home to me and the children – which was a very reassuring thing to hear.'

Sue: 'Well, all his protestations of innocence just added to your guilt really, because you felt guilty for doubting him, but he was actually lying to you, and that made you feel more guilty.'

Elizabeth: 'It did . . . yes it did . . . and I think there's this need to feel "If it's me, then I can do something about it, but if it's him then it's out of my hands." '

Sue: 'Yes, that's right . . . you feel as if you've got some control if it's your fault, and you take the blame.'

Elizabeth: 'Yes. We had a really massive row when he said he was going to collect our daughter's christening gown. He's got a mobile, and he wasn't home until eleven, having said he'd be home at 9pm. My two youngest were ill. I'd just had a terrible night of it, and I was worried sick, because I thought he had been in an accident, because he hadn't phoned, so when he came through the door, I just lost my temper with him. As soon as he came in I asked him "Why didn't you phone?" I felt dreadful . . . I remember saying to him "You might as well be dead, you're never here." He looked at me and said, "Well, I was happy until I came through the door." And I ended up apologising to him. What he'd actually done was pick up our daughter's christening gown, and then gone on and seen his lover, which I only found out later.'

Sue: 'Yes, I see . . . so he'd put the guilt onto you.'

Elizabeth: 'Yes, he'd put the guilt onto me . . . but also I felt, how could he do that? That was a special occasion . . . that was *our* daughter . . . he'd gone to pick up our baby's christening gown, and then gone on to see her. Somebody said to me "I wonder if she saw the christening gown before you did." '

Sue: 'That's terrible.'

Elizabeth: 'Yes, well . . . probably it didn't happen . . . but the point is, it's such deceit, and it's throwing it all back at me, you know.'

Sue: 'Yes, I know – to make you feel guilty . . . to make you take the blame when it must have been a really difficult time anyway. How did it come about then that he actually left the marital home?'

Elizabeth: 'Well, our daughter was christened, and two days later he came in, and I knew he didn't look right, and I said to him was he tired, and I was concerned about him, and did he need to see a doctor. I asked him if he was having a breakdown, and he said, "I don't know – perhaps I do need to see the doctor." And then he said he might just go away for the night first of all. He said, "I need some time to think" and I panicked. I thought, I've got a four year old, a two year old, and a three month old baby, and I can't understand why he's being like this. I talked to him, and he said he was being ridiculous . . . and I remember saying to him time and time again, "We could be so happy, but we've got to talk, and all you'll say to me is that you're being selfish, and you will change." I told him "It's not just you, there must be things about me you don't like", and he said, "No, you're fine." But he didn't mean that – basically it was "I don't want to talk about this." Do you see what I mean? "I don't want to talk about this, be quiet." '

And then he said he wasn't going to go, he was being silly and he was going to stay with us, and he didn't need time to think, this was what he wanted. I must admit, I felt very emotional and eventually we went to bed. It was gone midnight, and then the phone rang. It was a woman, and she said, "could she speak to Rick", and when I asked her who was calling she said she was a friend, so I passed the phone over to him, and he kept saying "It'll be all right – it'll be all right, look I'll ring you tomorrow, it'll be all right." When he put the phone down I said to him, "You're having an affair". He said "No, I'm not having an affair. It's just somebody at work and she's having problems with her husband, and he's been hitting her and she's had a big row with him, and I told her to call me any time, and so she called." I said I thought it was a bit strange she chose a male colleague to ring, but I added, "We must put her up if she's in trouble." They must have had a real laugh about that one!'

Sue: 'So after this obviously very distressing night for you, what actually happened in the mechanics of the thing? Did he then own up and move out?'

Elizabeth: 'No. What happened was . . . I was really tearful the next morning and very shaky, and I remember really sobbing with him there in the bedroom. I remember, he said words, but they didn't really mean anything, you know? But he said he wasn't having an affair, and I believed him.'

Sue: 'You want to believe them, don't you?'

Elizabeth: 'Yes, I desperately wanted to believe him. He went to work and at midday he rang and said, "Oh bad news, I've got to work late tonight. I've got to go away so I'll come home and get a shirt." I had said to him in the morning that obviously we would put her up if she needed a place to go, but to just be careful because . . . you know, I wanted him to be friends with her, I didn't want him to let her down if she needed a place to go and needed friendship, but I just felt very wary. He said that he would make that clear to her. So he came back to get his shirt . . . I knew her name was Felicity, and he volunteered this information. He said "Oh by the way I've spoken to Felicity and made it very clear to her that I don't really want anything to do with her affairs at all", and I said to him, "You mustn't be cruel and turn your back on her." But he said he'd made it very clear to her. And I can remember I just felt really tearful . . . I felt so uncertain . . . I just didn't know what was going on, and I started to cry and he put his arm round me . . . and then he went. Wednesday night he didn't come home, Thursday night one of the children had taken the phone off the hook, so he rang my sister and said he couldn't come home because he had to see some more doctors, and then Friday it got to half past seven, and I rang him on his mobile phone, and then he told me. He told me that what I suspected was true, he was having an affair, and he didn't want to be with me any more, he wanted to be with her.'

Sue: 'So that must have felt like the bottom had dropped out of your world.'

Elizabeth: 'It did. But then on the other hand there was a strange feeling of relief . . . I wasn't going mad. Because I'd actually got to the point where I was going to the doctor and telling her I was not thinking straight. Even my mother had said to me "You know he *does* care, you're not being fair", 'cos I got so desperate I said to my mother in the end, "I'm not sure he really loves me." I mean, he lied to her.'

Sue: 'He lied to everybody really . . .'

Elizabeth: 'Yes, but *I* felt I was going mad, and I felt so guilty . . . I wasn't the perfect wife, and things like that. But you know, you feel guilty for the slightest little thing. And I would think "If only I'd . . . if only I'd". In the first few months of him being away, I had so many "if only's" . . . all the time.'

Sue: 'But that is actually how they *try* to make you feel, consciously or not. They're actually putting the blame on to us because they can't face up to it themselves. That's actually what happens in these circumstances. That's not an uncommon thing at all.'

Elizabeth: 'No . . . he said to me that he didn't know if I wanted him to come home again. As he hadn't taken many things with him, he came home and packed a few things. I can remember just sitting there with him, holding the baby in my arms . . . and because he did *all* the finances, I asked him to show me exactly what was what. So . . . he did, in a very calm cool way. And then he walked out of the door, and I remember noticing he was taking his front door keys with him. I asked him for them, he seemed surprised, but he gave them to me . . . and he drove away. And in the next month or so, *I* packed up his belongings and *I* gave them to him.'

Sue: 'Did you ask him before he left, why he had drawn out his leaving for so long?'

Elizabeth: 'Yes, I did. He told me he ". . . wanted to keep his options open." And later he said that he couldn't be bothered to try. He left it to me to tell the children. I said "Are you going to say goodbye to them?" He went upstairs to them, but didn't spend very long . . . and that was it . . . he went.'

Sue: 'How long ago was that?'

Elizabeth: 'Over two years ago. He does see the children . . . he comes every other weekend, and takes them out for four to six hours . . . he cancels when it doesn't suit him. He does everything that's politically correct, but he doesn't ask about how they are emotionally or physically, and has made it clear that his involvement with them is confined to his visits.'

Sue: 'Can I ask you something about the Christian side of things? Would you say that your husband was an active Christian within your marriage? I know *you* were, but would you say that of him?'

Elizabeth: 'No. He didn't like going to church really.'

Sue: 'Did that cause any tension at all between you? Or was he happy for you to go?'

Elizabeth: 'At the time I thought he was happy for me to go. I would like to have believed it was because he felt it was right for me, but I think it was because I took the children with me and he got space in the house to himself . . . which is OK, because he did need space for himself . . . I mean, everybody does and that's fine. He did used to come along sometimes to church, but only if I asked him to.'

Sue: 'So when he left you, did you find the people within your church were a support to you?'

Elizabeth: 'I wasn't really *that* involved with the church. I did it for me.'

Sue: 'So who was your main support?'

Elizabeth: 'Linda, our lady curate was absolutely marvellous – absolutely marvellous, and kept me together actually. She really did. She was wonderful . . . and she had understanding, and wisdom. She helped me immensely . . . I don't find it that easy to open up.'

Sue: 'But maybe the fact that she was a woman priest helped.'

Elizabeth: 'It did.'

Sue: 'It wouldn't have been so easy to open up to a man?'

Elizabeth: 'No, it wouldn't. And I also think talking about when your husband has left you for another woman, it's very loaded, for many people . . . and it comes with unspoken judgements. And to actually be able to talk openly to somebody else who has not been through it, and is not judgemental, and does not the have that superior attitude of "Well, it would never happen to me. " . . .'

Sue: 'That's right. And also to someone who has the depth of understanding that Linda, the curate, has. She's actually helped *me* tremendously too. You do *need* somebody at the time, who you feel really understands.'

Elizabeth: 'Yes, and I think just to talk with her . . . I began to start the process of grieving, which I needed, instead of that numbness that protects.'

Sue: 'Because she was beside you in it?'

Elizabeth: 'Yes, I always knew she was only at the end of the phone, and she would come, and she was just *such* a support.'

Sue: 'Yes, well Linda's a very special person.'

Elizabeth: 'And I think somebody who . . . I could talk to about the children, and although she hasn't got children of her own . . . I know she used to teach . . . but I could talk to her and I felt she *really* understood. Because you see, my real agony . . . yes, I've agonised for me . . . but my *real* agony is for my children.'

Sue: 'Because they're so young?'

Elizabeth: 'Yes, and because they want a "Daddy" so much. Last year my sister's house group very kindly paid for us to go on holiday. Their love and care meant a great deal to us. We had a very happy time.'

Sue: 'That's lovely. Your mother too has helped you tremendously, hasn't she?'

Elizabeth: 'She's been wonderful. Since this has all happened, she has been so generous with her time and herself. The children love her deeply and so do I. It has brought us much closer together.

There have been occasions in the past when my

husband has lost his temper – especially with our eldest son – and that would be within about ten minutes of him coming into the house, and I've been frightened . . . that was towards the end of the marriage, and obviously he was under an awful lot of strain. I remember saying to my son on the way home from nursery school – and the nursery teacher had said to me that my son had positively sparkled since my husband had left – I said to him "How do you feel now that Daddy is not living with us any more?" And he said, "OK" I said to him, "Daddy's changed. He doesn't love me any more. He loves Felicity, and he wants to live with her now." And he said, "Will they get married and have children?" I said, "Maybe." He said, "OK" And I wanted to get past this "OK? Fine." He was very protective of me.'

Sue: 'But maybe he needed you to say it *wasn't* OK for you?'

Elizabeth: 'Exactly. I said to him, "Well, Mummy feels sad and angry sometimes that Daddy isn't living with us any more. Do you feel sad and angry?' And he said, "No, Mummy. I feel happy." I can remember we were crossing the road at the time – and I said, "Why do you feel happy?" And he said, "Well Daddy wasn't always that kind to me, Mummy.' And I thought, how true. But since then that has been swept away because Daddy comes, and Daddy takes him out to nice places. I know my eldest son is disillusioned with his father – he said to me, "Daddy lies" – but he'd told me Daddy lied before Daddy left us. In fact, when I think about it, my four year old was telling me "Daddy is lying", even though he didn't understand Daddy was having an affair.'

Sue: 'Well, they do know the difference between truth and lies at that age.'

Elizabeth: 'But the one thing my husband used to get really angry about was if *he* told a lie!'

Sue: 'Yes, well it's always the faults which are in your-self that you dislike most in other people.'

Elizabeth: 'But my husband used to get so angry if my son told a lie. I reminded him of this after he'd left and he said "I don't want him to grow up like me"!'

Sue: 'That's very perceptive! How have you felt about God during all this time – and now as well. How did your Christian faith help you? Or were you very angry with God?'

Elizabeth: 'Before my husband left, but when I knew something was terribly, terribly wrong, I can remember being in church and praying that we could work it out and find happiness together and I remember once I started to cry, and my sister put her arm around me and asked me what was wrong. And I couldn't tell her because I felt it would be dis-loyal. I tried *so* hard to make it work, but it was impossible – God hadn't answered the prayer the way I wanted it answered. But although things *are* a struggle, I've come to know Jesus in a way I wouldn't have been able to.'

Sue: 'More deeply?'

Elizabeth: 'Yes. My husband resented me going to church – I'm sure he did. That's not to say that mar-riage between a Christian and non-Christian can't work, I believe it can and does work. With Rick and myself, I think basically it came down to the fact that our principles in life had become so very different.'

Sue: 'So in a way, when he went, that tension had gone for you, and you could feel freer perhaps?'

Elizabeth: 'I did. On the one hand it was like a great big weight lifting – on the other hand it was like a living nightmare. I can remember driving the car and saying to God, "I realise You couldn't give me what I wanted, because it wasn't what my husband wanted, but in one way You've released me" '.

Sue: 'It always comes back to the fact that it takes two people in a marriage to make it work.'

Elizabeth: 'Yes, it does. And I was committed – but he wasn't.'

Sue: 'How would you say, two and a half years on, your relationship with God is? Because I *do* know that your husband has been extremely difficult – would you say that your relationship with God is deeper because of all this?'

Elizabeth: 'Yes. I *know* He's there. I know He's *always* there, and He sees me through the darkest places. And when I've felt utter despair – the only thing that's kept me going is my children. And my baby kept me going because she's so helpless, she's dependent on me for everything.

Just the knowledge that God is there, and that He isn't going to leave me, even if I turn my back on Him. Sometimes I have got extremely angry with God, and I think He understands that.'

Sue: 'If I was somebody in the same position you were two and a half years ago, and you had one thing to say to me, what would it be?'

Elizabeth: 'It depends what sort of mood they're in, but things *do* sort themselves out. A part of them will always be damaged, but it *does* get better. About God, however bad it feels, I would say, "He's there" '.

Chapter Twelve

OTHER PEOPLE'S STORIES (IV)

Robert

Robert is an Anglican vicar who was married for twenty-five years. His wife left him after an affair with another man. He speaks here with great depth and honesty of some of the problems faced by 'clergy couples' within their marriages.

Sue: 'Robert, you were married for twenty-five years, and you had children, didn't you?'

Robert: 'Yes, we had three children, two boys and a girl. I was twenty-five years old when I married and . . . it was a whirlwind romance, which looked very good . . . we married far too quickly.'

Sue: 'So you didn't really feel that you knew your wife terribly well before you were married. What would you say, if you can say anything, first made you realise that something was not quite right in your marriage?'

Robert: 'Um . . . difficult anyhow, because obviously we're two quite different personalities. I suppose I was totally inexperienced with regard to the whole idea of marriage. I come from a very masculine background – army life, I have no sisters, so I think I was just not very understanding about women and things, very much out of my background really. So that put me at quite a disadvantage, but at the same time it made me make as much effort as I could to try and understand and comprehend the other side of marriage and the difficulty with my wife. She was very insecure without me there and was somewhat dependent on me in a way, and I didn't understand at the time.'

Sue: 'It sounds to me as if you took most of the blame . . . do you think you did?'

Robert: 'No, I don't think I took the blame for what happened. I think considering our two separate stories, in some ways she was looking for things which I wasn't able to provide and I was trying to achieve something which perhaps was unrealistic as well.'

Sue: 'When you noticed that something was wrong, and you've already said you tried to understand your wife's side, did you admit to each other that there was something wrong?'

Robert: 'Well, it started, you know . . . she got attracted by another man, and in some ways I went along with that because I know it's very difficult being a clergy wife. She needed recreation and wished to go out with this person as a friend – a mutual friend of all of us – and I think she became increasingly concerned for him, more than friendship. Then she had a job and worked with him quite a bit in a part-time role, and that obviously gave them the opportunity to increase their relationship. It was a slippery slope.'

Sue: 'By the time you realised it, it was too late?'

Robert: 'That's right. She always used to say what a hell of a thing it is to be a clergy wife and so on, and I said, "Well, I understand that, and therefore it's right that you should have your life and be involved in as little or as much in the church as you wish." '

Sue: 'So when you married, were you already a clergyman?'

Robert: 'No, I wasn't. When we got married, we moved into a change of vocation, which was quite challenging for her and me, but she was very supportive. She worked, and supported me in the years of training.'

Sue: 'So was she a Christian herself?'

Robert: 'Not as deeply as I would hope or expect – nominally, I think. Again, this is one of the great regrets, that we never really shared intimately in the Christian faith. I think she felt it very much as a threat. Some people say that to be a clergy wife is to be married to a bigamist, in the sense that you've got to share the clergy person with the Lord, and so if you feel that you can't take that in your stride and understand that completely, then the church and the Lord become a rival for your affection; there's no doubt about it, the Lord does demand the intimate side of a person's life inevitably, and that's what vocation is, isn't it? But it's so easy for a wife or a husband to resent this, and once you get into that you're vulnerable to all the sorts of upsets and hurts; I mean it's a career obviously, being a clergy family, with a lot of hurts and disappointments, no money, and difficulties to be encountered. Then it's so easy for a marriage in a clergy family to deteriorate for that reason.'

Sue: 'Yes, almost without realising how bad it's getting. I loved being a clergy wife, but the stresses were just as great even though I did love it and my faith was, if anything, stronger than my husband's – but it was still enormously stressful.'

Robert: 'Yes, I think . . . on the other hand I take the view that the Christian faith is not to be imposed in any way. It's something that people are liberated into, and so I was very gentle to encourage her in her faith, but not forceful because I think that would have been wrong. But it did become a rival.'

Sue: 'Another lover really, wasn't it?'

Robert: 'Yes it was. But I thought that in a sense it might help things on – she had this job with the other man who was involved in her work and they had quite a good team relationship. I thought,

"Well, this is good, it's a change from the vicarage, and it gives her something different, and gives her a sort of liberation." I thought it might, given time, sort of come round. But it didn't of course, it just got slowly, slowly worse.'

Sue: 'By that stage did you feel there was anything you could do about it?'

Robert: 'Well, yes. It was very stressful for her and me, and I did suggest counselling. She didn't accept that very well, so I went and had counselling and she got very stressed up about all this. She became a very stress-laden person, which made me even more tender about how to handle it. Again, I don't think I had the skill to pull it round really.'

Sue: 'Would you say – and I certainly felt this – that by this stage it's almost too late anyway, but for it *not* to be too late, you do actually need a third person to help you both?'

Robert: 'Yes. Well, she wouldn't accept that, but what held us together was commitment to the youngish family we had and working for them, and I must admit she was a very good mother, and ran the home, and was a very good vicar's wife too. The parish thought very highly of her. She was very compassionate, had a lot of qualities, but nonetheless this great feeling of resentment, deep hurts. What hurts we had never seemed to heal. There was more stored up and more resentment, and eventually she felt that she had to go, so she connived it in such a way that she left home and took a new job and we went our separate ways. We did this very graciously and I was happy to do that – the family were quite well cared for in this regard.'

Sue: 'So in that way it wasn't, so far as the family were concerned, what you'd call an acrimonious break?'

Robert: 'Not really, no. Again I think you see, love is a matter of giving people freedom to grow and develop. Maybe that's too much of a hands-off approach, but that's the line I took, that gentleness, patience, understanding, forbearance, endurance, all these sorts of things, was the way to handle it, rather than force it one way or another. That wouldn't have worked, obviously.'

Sue: 'Looking back – I know you can't act at the time with hindsight – but looking back, would you have done anything differently to try and keep your marriage together?'

Robert: 'I don't think so. I know it sounds like projecting it all on the other side, but she made impossible demands on me. I was in a constant dilemma, demands at home and demands at work, and I think she would have liked me to be a person who made one's vocation second or third priority . . . but I am a person of vocation . . . maybe I work too hard . . . not enough time for the family . . . yes, I've done all that!'

Sue: 'Do you think if you'd been a solicitor or a dentist, things could have been different?'

Robert: 'I've often thought that! She thought I could be a clergyman like a dentist, set hours, that sort of thing. She would have preferred that, but I don't think it would have ultimately resolved things.'

Sue: 'Do you think the church has got a bigger role to play in caring for its clergy marriages?'

Robert: 'Yes and no. The bishop sends a nice letter every year saying, "The following people are counsellors; if you've got problems these are the people to approach." In fact that's what I did, and it worked very well; but I would say that I think clergy need a lot more care than they get – maybe not at a bishop level – maybe more at a rural dean level.'

Sue: 'My own husband wouldn't approach any of these counsellors because they were all connected with the church, and he was afraid that if he said, "I'm having an affair with a parishioner,' it might get back to the powers that be. I think that was one of his biggest problems.'

Robert: 'Yes, I understand – that's rather different because the boot was on the other foot really. I think the church should be more supportive, but for my wife the worm of resentment had got going, and the church was part of the problem for her, not the answer.'

Sue: 'But when you got married and you weren't a clergyman, did she know you were going to be one?'

Robert: 'She did in a way, and she consented to it. But you do get knocks in the church, and we did – several big ones.'

Sue: 'I knew my husband was going to be a clergyman when we married, so I thought I knew what was involved because I'd seen my own parish priest. The reality was a completely different thing. It's simply not true to say you know what's going to happen, because there's no way on earth you can.'

Robert: 'Well, both of us were like this. She didn't come from a church family at all, and I was an army officer and had no idea about it all either.'

Sue: 'What would you say is your chief regret?'

Robert: 'Now it's a long way back . . . there were a lot of good things about our marriage, and I've tried to forget the painful things. I've learnt a lot through it; it drove me to pave new ways through the pain of it all; I had to work that out – spiritually and theologically. I found my faith exceedingly helpful. To cope with those sorts of thing without a faith, without a living Lord would be well nigh impossible, it seems to me inconceivable. So in some ways it was an enriching experience, though a painful one.'

Sue: 'So what would you want to say to a clergy couple who found themselves in a similar position?'

Robert: 'Well, I have to say, first of all, you have to proceed prayerfully, that is crucial. The trouble is, what stops you praying is the pain and the resentment you may have against the Lord for putting you in this position. You can easily think, having endured all sorts of marital pain, there's a great sense of injustice, failure and broken expectations, ruining a career, and these sorts of things, and you can blame God very powerfully – and that's what you must *not* do. That is what the devil would like you to do.'

Sue: 'So you don't think God's big enough to take the blame . . .?'

Robert: 'If you want to blame God, you *can*, but for goodness sake don't put God in Coventry and let a hatred barrier build up between yourselves and the Lord. What I would say is that the Lord *does* understand, and He is compassionate, and He *will* see you through it. But of course if you are party to a clergy divorce, either husband or wife, you could so easily blame the Lord, and not even look in the direction of a spiritual answer, and you can get quite an anti-God feeling. That's the big danger. Don't let a broken marriage separate you from God. Rather let Him come to you and let Him minister to you in the confusion and the pain, and don't doubt that. So go for it spiritually, inwardly, and don't be separated out – that's the first and foremost advice, I would say.

And secondly, yes, it's terribly important to have Christian friends and people to offload to, and maybe counselling and help – I found that very helpful. It gave me a deeper understanding and a deeper sense of . . . well, from understanding comes a sense of forgiveness and coping and just the sheer fact that you are able to offload. But again, this is very difficult. A lot of clergy don't have spiritual directors or people they can readily turn to. Obviously they feel they must keep these things out of the parish circulation, then where are you? We're very isolated people, clergy and clergy families. OK, you can resort to the people on the list in the envelope the bishop or archdeacon gives you. Again it takes a lot of courage to go to your bishop and say, "Look, I've got a real problem here, and I want to tell you about it." I had to grasp that nettle, and I'm glad to say the bishops were very understanding, very helpful and they got quite involved, and they were very supportive – as much as they could be. So if you can, do share and be open about it. The other thing clergy are bound to think is that it harms their career prospects and things like that – I don't think necessarily it does, not in this day and age. I think things have changed. Sad to say, there are so many clergy marriages that have been through these experiences.'

Sue: 'The honesty in admitting that you need help and going for it, would I imagine, be more in your favour than trying to "sweep it under the carpet".'

Robert: 'Yes, I think so . . .'

Sue: 'And also, the experience itself will help in your understanding of others?'

Robert: 'Yes, it can. And you *can* survive. That's the other thing. There is survival. There is new life beyond these things.'

Sue: 'You're saying, there is life after divorce?'

Robert: 'Yes . . . I've been through an awful mincing in some respects but then strangely enough, the grace of God has turned it into valid experience, valid lessons for life, and I think I'm a wiser and more compassionate pastor as a result of all these things. It's taught me a lot about theology and suffering. So it *can* have a creative effect on you.'

Sue: 'Would you say that you have learnt to embrace the paradox of pain, that life can hurt and go on hurting; and yet, our loving God is still in control?'

Robert: 'Yes, certainly. God doesn't promise us no hurts and pain, but what He does promise is to be with us and to share. That may seem a poor consolation, but it gets you a long way along, definitely.

And the other thing I think clergy are awfully haunted by, is a sense of failure. They're meant to be the role models for their parishes, and things like that and you can feel, "Well, what sort of example is this to my people?" But again, I think the good news is, parishioners are a lot wiser and more perceptive than you ever give them credit for. My people have watched it all over a period of years. They very silently and discreetly, prayed and cared all the way through. We've never talked about these things, but they have been very supportive. Certainly they haven't been anti or critical, or rubbed my nose in it in any way at all. If anything I've found people to be very compassionate. You know, "poor old Robert, he's having a very trying time in the vicarage, but we'll care for him and encourage him" – and there's something exceedingly beautiful in that, and again I found that was enriching in some way.'

Sue: 'So in fact it can be a very positive thing, because they realised that priest or not, you're actually a man and just as fragile as them?'

Robert: 'That's right . . . earthen vessels. It is a disaster of a particular nature, particularly it's a failing in love, and I suppose we're meant to be the experts in love and relationships. That's what the Christian religion is all about, our relationship with God, and our relationship with one another being wholesome and holy and good, then you can find yourself, and though you would aspire to all these things, in agony and an awful mess, you certainly don't feel the expert. Strangely enough, through the chastening experience and the affliction of it all, you *do* become the expert. You understand how people work – anger and inner pain and grief and hopelessness. All these things are part of our humanity just as much as our hands, feet and fingernails are.'

Sue: 'And I suppose you learn, like I did, that God is more interested in our failures than our successes.'

Robert: 'Yes, I think our witness as clergy – I know it may sound a bit pious, but our witness is very simply, that our Lord has been with us in the conflict, in the affliction. Not that we've won, not that we've succeeded, not that we've done any of these things, but our witness is that the Lord's been with us and that has proved to be a great consolation, a great blessing and a great truth, because we know that when other occasions of weakness and brokenness come, that same presence of the Lord will be there. And of course *life* will lead to more and more brokenness, and eventually suffering and death anyhow. To know the Lord is your companion in all these things is vitally important, and of course the church holds this treasure. For example we must say, "Look what *Jesus* is doing for me in the affliction", rather than, "Look at this vicar with a broken marriage." '

Sue: 'So what you've done with it is more important than what's happened?'

Robert: 'Well, what God has done. That's our task isn't it, to point people to God, not to whether I've succeeded or failed, or whether I'm whole or broken.'

Sue: 'So look what He can do with our failings?'

Robert: 'Yes, that's it exactly.'

Chapter Thirteen

ACCEPTANCE AND FORGIVENESS?

*'Let me see the past times as a gift from God that many
people never know . . . '*
Quote from 'Brenda', whose story
appears in Chapter Nine.

Don't shut the book! Please! There will be some I know,
who have already looked down the list of chapter
headings, seen 'Acceptance and Forgiveness?' and put
the book back on the shelf! Maybe they have not
noticed the question mark at the end . . . ! I am *not* going
to tell you that we must 'forgive and forget'. Nor am I
going to say that we must glibly accept all that has happened to us and then quote Romans 8 v 28 at you. If I
were to do that, the very best thing you could do with
this book would be to seek me out and throw it at me!

There is an awful lot in the Bible about forgiveness.
And of course, ultimately we know that we must reach
a point of forgiveness because the teaching in the Bible
is so clear. But I do not pretend to understand it, and I
do not pretend to know how we deal with our feelings
when the pain is new and very raw – except perhaps
that at this stage we can only feel them, that's all. All
we can say then is 'I don't want to forgive. Why should
I? Look what she/he has done to me.' It certainly
didn't help me when 'helpful' friends pointed out that
because of verses like Matthew chapter 6 verses 14-15,
we must instantly forgive. 'For if you forgive men for
their transgressions, your heavenly Father will also forgive you.' I find it impossible to believe in a God whose

forgiveness is dependent on our willingness to forgive others. His grace is much bigger than that, and His gifts are free – not conditional. And I don't advise we go around quoting this verse to others who have recently been deserted by their spouses. If we do that, then we will deserve everything they may say to us! I think the secret of forgiveness is time. But I am jumping ahead.

When I first thought about this chapter, I called it 'Forgiveness and Acceptance'. But I changed it around when a friend pointed out to me that without acceptance, we cannot forgive. In all honesty I haven't yet finished thinking that one through, but I'm sure she's right! It *sounds* right, and the more I think about it the more it seems that without acceptance, there are many things that cannot happen. Things like forgiveness, for without acceptance we will still be resenting the place we are in, consequently where there is resentment, there cannot be wholehearted forgiveness.

Without acceptance we cannot move forward, because resentment shackles us to the past. Acceptance is the key which turns the lock on the padlock that fastens the chains which hold us to the past. We cannot say 'What next?', and 'If only this, or this hadn't happened . . .' at the same time, because if we do then we choke on our own bitterness. One lesson I learnt very early on is that resignation and forgiveness are not the same thing.

Acceptance is an active thing – not passive. Being passive implies resignation. Acceptance is positive – resignation is negative. A sitting back kind of fatalism – 'What will be, will be'. It is stagnant and doesn't grow. Resignation and acceptance do not make good bedfellows – in fact, they don't even live in the same house!

Acceptance moves to embrace life – goes out to meet it almost; it moves, and because it moves, it grows. Growth without maturity *is* possible – but an acceptance which is based in the love of God, not only

181

grows, it matures. This, written in a few short sentences, may look and sound very easy. But *real* acceptance is never easy – it is a fighting, clawing, sometimes crawling on our knees thing. It is often one step forward and two back! Within acceptance there is never room for complacency. It is something at which we continually need to work – it is not a point at which we arrive. Acceptance is not a moment in time – it is a way of living. Resignation and acceptance are poles apart. It is the difference between shrugging our shoulders – or raising our hands in greeting. The difference between nodding at someone when you meet them – or embracing them. The difference between walking away – or joining in the dance; between a shut book – or an open one, between a blank page – or one on which we write. Resignation is the tired bud which withers and dies – acceptance the lovely flower which slowly unfolds, spreading its perfume for all to share. Between resignation and acceptance there is a battle, with suffering as the cavalry, and humility bringing up the rear. Not a false 'poor little me, I am worth nothing' humility, but a realisation of our own worth in God's eyes, and of His all embracing greatness; a knowledge of His enormity and His world – of our littleness and our place in that world.

I spent four years after my husband had left this last time, feeling, not exactly bitter but still angry enough to keep looking back. I felt – and still do on some days – a great and almost unbearable sadness for what was, what had been. I wanted so much to have it all back, to be back in the past with the husband I love and for the past to be *now*. But I found that as I tried to build a new life, at the same time, I had to find a way to stop doing that. It is impossible to walk forward, when our heads are screwed round looking back over our shoulders. I did that, and I fell over, because I couldn't see where I was going! The past and the future are *not* realities. The past is gone, and the future hasn't happened yet. The only reality for any of us is the present moment. NOW is what matters. Sure, the past helped to shape what we are now, but like the wind, it is gone forever, and until Dr Who becomes reality and we develop a time machine, we can't get it back!

I would like to be able to write here that I received counselling, and friends ministered and prayed for me, and suddenly and miraculously I found I could accept where I was now – the time and the place. But if I wrote that, it would be untrue, because it didn't happen like that.

First, I had to learn that acceptance comes in two parts. Number one is accepting everything that has happened to me. I had a big problem here, because everything that had happened to me was screamingly, terribly and frighteningly unfair. And that made it difficult to accept. So I asked myself why that was. I came up with the simple answer that I wanted life to be fair. If we're honest, we all do. Because if life and events are unfair to us, then the word 'injustice' starts hammering around in our brains. If something is unfair, therefore unjust, then it's out of our control, and it usually means we have been misunderstood too. And that's frightening. We all – Christian and non-Christian alike – love to control our own lives. We talk grandly about 'God being in control if my life', and we may let Him sit beside us on the driving seat – but *we* hold the reins! I know *I* do that. I say one thing – convince myself I really mean it, and partly I do, but not completely. God can be the head, but I want to be the neck that turns that head!

I can give you a personal, recent example. During the writing of this chapter, I was given a month 'off sick' by my GP. For the first two weeks I felt far too ill to even think about writing, and much too exhausted to even turn on my word processor! I had to resign from a job I loved. I felt it was the only thing I could do, given the circumstances. Let me share with you now some of the thoughts and feelings I experienced during my illness.

'At the moment I am in a transition stage; something which because of all the changes forced on me by my recent past, I find very difficult to handle. But I *do* believe God is in control of my life, and now, in a very real way, I have to "put my money where my mouth is"! I have to believe, as a good friend said to me two days ago, that God goes before me, and He has in the past too. At the moment it feels, as that same perceptive friend said, "like a burden which is simply too heavy to bear". But I must give God my grief for the past, and my trust for the future. That makes sense of the "sacrament of the present moment". By giving Him my yesterdays and trusting Him with my tomorrows, I can live my today in the knowledge of His guidance and love. What has happened is grossly unfair and unjust, but I think I have really gotten hold of the plain and simple fact that life is not fair. If we continue to expect it to be, we shall continually be disappointed. And it doesn't matter if things have been unfair for years, we have no heavenly immunity because we're Christians. If we trip out our catalogue of disasters to all and sundry in the world, we won't get, "There, there, dear, oh how sad, how *unfair!*" We're far more likely to get, "Tough, you think you've got problems . . . it's a hard world!" No, like so many people, I have got to "lift myself up, dust myself down, and start all over again!" I *do* believe God will give me a future, a new career, and all the things I need to live. He has after all, a very good track record in my life to date – He and I have been through some pretty tough times together and He's always come up trumps in the past, so I have no reason to doubt Him now. And knowing that He knows just how unfair it all is at the moment, gives me great consolation.'

So – the first part of acceptance is accepting the things that have happened in the past – and this is the really important bit, LEAVING THEM THERE. Having done that, we can then move on to accepting our present place. The situation we are in now. And that's the key word, because our todays lay the foundation for our tomorrows. I don't want to keep looking back. I find it so *very* much easier to walk with my eyes looking forward. If God had meant us to keep looking back, we'd have eyes in the back of our heads as well! The reason we haven't is because to see two places at once would be too confusing, and we'd get giddy and fall over – just like I used to!

The 'sacrament of the present moment' is a lovely thing to practise. It's hard, but very rewarding. Put incredibly simply, it's embracing with everything that we are, *this moment* in time, living it to the full, but more than that – concentrating all our energies into it and offering it to God as a sacrifice. He has given us this moment, this day, this life, and *whatever* happens to us, He *can* and does use it for good. What we need to do is to live it as a sacrament, with humour certainly, but also with reverence and respect – not regret and longing for something else.

A few years ago when I worked at The Old Rectory at Crowhurst, the Churches Ministry Of Healing Centre, I started my time there, as everyone else did then, on the house team. One day I was asked to clean the wax off the carpet in the chapel. I was kneeling under the altar when it suddenly struck me where I was. I remember saying silently to God, 'This is *Your* house, and I'm under *Your* altar, where *Your* body is broken, and *Your* blood poured out – for the world, and for me. Please take my cleaning of this carpet as an offering of love, given in all humility to You to use as You choose.' I made my movements reverent and graceful as befits Almighty God. I felt both humbled and uplifted. It took me quite a while to do it, and suddenly a woman's voice said, 'Thank you, my dear, you have just preached the most eloquent sermon I have ever heard.' I had not seen anyone in the chapel when I went in, and I was so surprised that I bumped my head on the altar as I looked out and saw a woman sitting right in the corner pew. She told me that she could see by my movements and attitude that I had given the task to God as an offering! I don't remember seeing her again amongst the guests, and I sometimes wonder . . . could I have 'entertained an angel unawares?'

As Benedictine Oblates we are encouraged 'to be the first to see Christ in the other', so for example whenever I clean stairs, I think of Christ's feet walking up them, for it's Him in each person who treads them. I can assure you that by doing this, it can transform the humblest task into the highest oblation. Try it – you may well be surprised!

There is another aspect of acceptance too. Perhaps the most important one. It comes at the height of the Eucharist – at that supreme most precious of all moments, when we take into ourselves the broken body of our Lord. By accepting His brokenness we are offering to Him our acceptance of our *own* brokenness – broken dreams, broken promises, and in some cases broken hearts too. By accepting the wine poured out for us, we are accepting the pouring out of His brokenness, taken into us, in the world. All our broken dreams and desires, our hopes and aspirations, our grief and our pain will be poured out and given as a sacramental offering to Him for the salvation of the world. He gives, we receive - then, and only then, as we go out into the world and our everyday lives, we give, and it is not our responsibility whether what we give is received or not. Sometimes the only gift we have to offer God the next time we come to the Eucharist is our own pain and brokenness at not being received. This is at the heart of Eucharist living, which is at one and the same time both costly and free. It cost God His only Son – whom He gave freely. It costs us the struggle to give our brokenness to Him, which when transformed by His love, we then freely give to others.

But acceptance is the key word. Without Christ's acceptance of God's will for Him there would be nothing for us to receive. Without our willingness to receive, we have nothing to give. At the Eucharist it would be useless if we did not either lift our hands, or open our mouths to receive the wafer or broken bread. The priest, God's representative on earth, would pass on to the next communicant and we would miss out, because we had not been willing to accept His gift and we would have nothing in our hearts to give to a needy world. If we do not drink the wine poured out for us, if we let it pass by, then we cannot be outpoured for the life of the world. Which brings us back to acceptance being an active not a passive thing.

God does not *give* pain and suffering, but because we live in a fallen world He has to allow us to partake in it. We cannot be in the world and not be touched by it. And just as we accept all that is good and lovely, so we have to learn to accept what is difficult and painful – and unfair, or we become bitter and 'unbalanced' people. I find it a source of immeasurable comfort that when I am suffering deeply, or in great pain, I know that God is suffering with me and He grieves because my heart is broken.

Just after I was first 'off sick' with my recent illness, I was sitting on my balcony saying the Benedictine office of Lauds. The sun was pouring through the trees in the garden – it was a bright July day, warm and balmy. A huge bee was busily investigating every flower for pollen on my fuchsias, which hung in profusion from my two hanging baskets. In the middle of a very difficult patch in my life, God reached down and touched me. I felt at peace, warm and content, and for a moment it felt like earth and heaven met in a place of 'otherness'. Then I saw it – the spider's web. Luckily it had no inhabitants, as like my younger daughter, I am a confirmed arachnaphobic! It glistened and shone in the sun, and I thought how beautiful it was – how clever, how fragile yet how strong. Then I realised – it was like our hearts, fragile, yet strong. On that sun drenched, hazy summer's morning I wrote the following

The Spider's Web And The Wounded Heart

It hung between two railings and shimmered gently
in the sun.
It moved and breathed, pulsated like a living
thing,
Within the breeze which made it lift and fall.

It must have been so strong to sustain the life
it held –
Which now was gone – leaving it vulnerable, empty and
exposed
– Like a fragile thread of silk it hung
– The spider's web.

It lay between the body and the soul –
It rose and fell to the rhythm of life.
It moved and breathed – a pulsating living thing
Within the body to which it gave the gift of life.

It must have been so strong to sustain the life
it gave
– Which, still being there, left it vulnerable,
open and exposed.
Like a fragile piece of silk, it lay –
The wounded heart.

One day it would be gone
The spider's web –
Its threads caught and carried on the wind –
And no one would know it had ever been –

For it would leave no marks to speak of its being.

One day it will heal
The wounded heart –
The pain caught and carried on the wind –
And only One would know it had ever been
But it will leave scars to speak of its being.

And it will be the same One who saw them both –
Who looked, and watched, and held the memory –
The One who formed them and holds each one
– The spider's web – and the wounded heart.

I thought an awful lot about forgiveness. Unfortunately I did not come up with a definitive answer! The one single answer someone *did* give me that helped me the most, was the one which shocked me the most! Maybe because it was the one thing I didn't expect anyone to say to me – I'm sure the answers Jesus gave shocked people, because He said many unexpected things too. I was talking a a dear friend of mine, someone I both love very much and also respect very much – Jennifer Rees Larcombe. She and I have much in common, and but for her constant support, never failing encouragement and love, and her real 'front line' prayers every day for me whilst writing this book, I think that on more than one occasion I would have given up, for it has not been an easy book to write.

One day when we were together, we were talking about forgiveness. Actually at that time I was not thinking about my husband and his mistress, but someone else very close to me who has wronged me very deeply in the past. I remember asking, 'How can I forgive him – he has damaged me so much – how can I forgive him?' Jen's answer was totally unexpected and shook me to the roots! She said, 'You can't. How can you be expected to forgive at this time. It's impossible and no amount of people telling you that you must, will alter your feelings.' One of the things I love most about Jen is her deceptively down to earth approach! I realised more and more in the days following that reply just how right she was. Everyone else had been saying I *had* to get to a point of forgiveness, making me feel that in the time until I could do that, I was a second class Christian – a bit less than all right! Now, here was this lovely Christian lady I respect so much, giving me permission to feel unable to forgive, yet making me feel OK about it into the bargain! What a weight was lifted off me that day. But of course she's right. If we *cannot* forgive, we cannot, and feelings don't change just because we think they should.

I know there is one school of thought which says (rather primly I always think), 'Set the mind in the right direction (whatever *that* is!), and the emotions will follow.' How do I feel about that statement? Sufficient to say, 'I wish, oh *how* I wish, it were that easy.' To the person who said it to me I would add, as politely as I could of course, '*You* stand in my place, watching the husband you love live with another man's wife who actively set out to steal him from you. And he allowed himself to be stolen, for it does after all "take two to tango!"' The feelings that generates are *so* powerful, and *so* destructive, and *so* consuming, that no trite clichés about 'setting the mind in the right direction' come anywhere near to even touching the tremendous and frightening depths of my pain. So one of us is wrong – either the cliché, or me . . . !?

Let me share with you the thoughts of my four friends who have so courageously shared their stories in the four chapters preceding this one. I asked them all the same questions regarding forgiveness. The first question was, 'Do you feel you have forgiven your spouse and the other person?' Their answers were as follows:

Brenda said simply, 'I have forgiven my spouse and his new wife.'

Christine answered, 'Until I pondered this question, I believed I had forgiven my husband, but as I realise I still harbour resentment, the answer must be "no".'

Elizabeth just stated with admirable honesty, 'No.'

Robert had more to say, 'Forgiveness. I have had a lot of thought on this. Forgiveness is the gateway to healing. That is why we are called by God to be a people of forgiveness. We all need to be healed . . . forgiveness can never be an option. It has to be attempted, like the healing of disease, or the fighting of fires. So where there is deep personal hurt or injury, forgiveness must be our aim. Firstly we have to work at understanding the situation . . . why am I hurt . . . what causes it . . . deep research into one's life and the lives of others, down the family trees and the surrounding social environments.

'Forgiveness without understanding is worthless and will not heal. Thus we have to ask God to reveal the truth to us in our search for understanding . . . this then enables us to forgive. Let's start with oneself before God . . . from there one progresses slowly to forgiveness of the other. Inwardly I have done this, and I have a large measure of peace in doing so. That said, it is something I have to revisit on and off to check as I move onto new perspectives of myself and my story.'

Next, I asked them all, 'If you have forgiven, how did you come to this? What helped or hindered you?'

Brenda said, 'It took a long period of time to come to that point, but after two years I was able, again after a lot of prayer, to forgive my husband. It came about because God bombarded me in my readings and my prayer time. I also know that until I was able to forgive, God could not begin the real healing in my life and that was how it proved to be. Suddenly, when I had spoken those words to my husband, and before other witnesses, things began to get better.

'The more difficult job was forgiving the lady. She had been a friend, a member of our church and fellowship, and I had a problem coming to terms with her being prepared to "steal" my spouse, especially as she had a husband of her own. However, I have been able to forgive her just recently after listening to yet another sermon on forgiveness. I was hindered by a feeling of revenge as far as the lady was concerned. I literally felt that I would do her some harm if I met her anywhere. So all this had to be dealt with before I could come to a state of forgiveness, both for myself and her.'

Robert said, 'Forgiveness is something which has to be studied. Read a few books on it. But far more importantly it has to be prayed through in dialogue with the Lord . . . as well as supportive friends. Also seeing it in action in other situations, between other people . . . whether they do, or don't. Seeing the effects of non-forgiveness can be very salutory. Christianity is all about love and forgiveness . . . how one copes without the richness of our heritage and faith I cannot understand.'

The next question I asked was, 'If you have not forgiven, what do you feel? Do you *want* to forgive?'

Christine answered to this, 'I am fully aware that I am punishing my husband by not forgiving him, and thereby feeding his need to feel guilty.'

Elizabeth said in answer to this question, 'Anger and disbelief that two people can behave in such a selfish, greedy and cruel way, with apparently no thought to the havoc and sheer pain they have and are causing their spouses and children. Rick said he loved us and cared for us, he had made his marriage vows as I had. I was always committed to him and our children; I thought he was committed too.

'He walked out on me and our three children (aged four, two and three months). I can't forgive him or her yet – I do hope to one day. My husband continues to choose to make life very difficult for us, both emotionally and financially. I totally accept he is with . . . – I do not wish him back.

'I could forgive him if he asked me to – if he was

192

truly sorry for all the hurt, and started to show he really cared about his children and, where he could, made life easier for me as a one parent family. But he behaves as if he is playing some sort of game. It's hard to communicate with someone who isn't dealing in realities – perhaps it's too difficult for him to do so.'

Finally I asked my four friends this question, 'Do you think that as Christians, it is our duty to forgive?'

Brenda said, 'I was tempted in the early days to think that as a Christian I had a duty to forgive. I now realise that this is a very dangerous thing to think. There can be no forgiveness unless it is truly meant from the bottom of my heart. It is also a continuous thing. I have to keep forgiving. Bitterness and resentment creep back into my thoughts and the only way to deal with it, is to first ask for forgiveness for myself from God, and then speak out forgiveness for these two people yet again. For quite a time I was convinced that it wasn't my job to forgive them, and I think that was right. But since then God has gently led me into a state of repentance for myself, and through that to be able to forgive. That has been an amazing release for me.'

Christine says, 'I believe it is the Christian duty to forgive; from the perspective of human frailty I know it is not that easy.'

Elizabeth says most movingly, 'I believe God would like me to forgive, but understands that at present I cannot. I'm quite happy for God to forgive them, but at the moment *I* cannot forgive – I am not ready yet.'

Robert's answer was as follows, 'Yes . . . yes . . . but only when the home work has been done. It must be our aim all the time. Yet the road to it is very hard, and must be worked at time and time again. Our desires for healing and new life all point to this landmark of forgiveness. It is the crest of the mountain, which must be scaled if we are ever to visit the new land beyond.'

Robert says, '. . . but only when the home work has been done.' Although I know exactly what he means, I found for myself, I couldn't approach the thing like preparation for a dissertation. *My* home work consisted mainly of waiting. Waiting, and constantly asking God to make me begin to want to forgive those two people who have robbed me of so much. One problem I have is that I am constantly reminded of what they did because *I* live with the enforced results of their actions on me, every moment of every day and night of my life as it is now. But *that* is where the acceptance part I wrote of earlier comes in. One cliché that is irritatingly true is, 'People only have the power over you that *you* give them.' Gosh, how I hate clichés, especially if they're true! But if I allow them to let me go on in hatred for her, and anger with them both, then not only have they robbed me of everything which made my life happy and good, but they would have turned me into a bitter and twisted person as well. And bitter and twisted people are usually friendless, unlovable, and end up destroying everything they touch, including themselves. Scott Peck, in his book *The Road Less Travelled*, speaks of just that. Two roads leading through a wood, and one is 'the road *less* travelled.' Bad news folks; or is it good news? The one travelled mostly is the one we can see any day of the week on our TVs. One of the joys(?) of being home in the day is being able to watch daytime TV! Watch some of the American 'chat' shows (although having sat utterly amazed through several of them, I think that name is a misnomer. They should be called 'shout' shows!), and you will see the other more travelled road in action. A high percentage of these shows is related to adultery and extra-marital affairs, with the people concerned doing their 'dirty washing in public.' They speak of their most intimate feelings, their sexual powers, or lack of them, in the most sickening and degrading detail. These tirades are usually greeted by rapturous applause and 'rounding off' remarks by the 'shout' show host/hostess which are both unctuous and obsequious! That's the road most travelled.

The 'the road less travelled' leads in time to forgiveness, and ultimately, to healing. I know which of the two I prefer – how about you?

Recently I was with Jennifer Rees Larcombe at her home nearby. I was feeling deeply unhappy and she simply held me as I wept and whispered words given to her, from God, for me. She said, '. . . you're giving Him the most precious gift you have to give Him – your pain, and He will use it for others. Don't give up – not now – keep going – don't give up . . . you're hanging on a cross for Him . . . hang there a little longer.' Knowing how close Jen is to our Lord I value her opinions very highly and those words helped me more than I can say, and indeed gave me the strength to keep going, and not give up.

I'd like to end this chapter on a positive note, and tell you what has, and *is* happening to me about forgiveness. I said I had no definitive answer – but the Christian life is never static, it is a journey, a transition from one point of learning to the next.

It is nearly five years now since I said 'Goodbye' to my husband for that final time. During most of that time I've badgered God about forgiveness. I've thrashed around, I've worried, and of course, I've prayed; then, after Jen's wise words – I've waited. Now I can truthfully say that I'm slipping gently into a part of forgiveness. Like many wronged wives, I guess forgiveness for 'the other woman' takes much longer, for we do not have the added dimension of love for them to help us, as we may have for our husbands. I am not completely there yet, so I shall not say that I am. But my God is so big, I know eventually He *will* bring me through. Remember Rilke's quote? 'Be patient towards all that is unresolved in your heart . . .' Be patient with yourselves. Just as in the Eucharist we watch and wait with the bread and wine, as they wait to be transformed by God's awesome power, let us too be content to give Him the broken pieces of our lives, and all the crumbs as well. And then let us wait with open hands and hearts for all that He has to change us into, and all that He has to give.

Forgive?
Me?
Them?

I can't Lord.
Can't do it.

Do I want to?
Do I?
Not even sure of that Lord.
Feel muddled.

Seems so hard.
Why should I forgive?
They have hurt me
So much.

They have taken everything
That is mine
And left me lying
In the dirt.

All I can say is
'Lord, help me to want to want
To forgive.'
And then –

You do the rest Lord –
You do the rest.

Chapter Fourteen

'PEEPING OUT' – LEARNING TO LIVE AGAIN

A Hint Of Dreams

Is this the prison of my mind
that casts dark shadows
on the wall beyond
and beckons invitingly
to forbidden lands?

Or is the heart strong enough
to turn the key – open the door
and release undreamt of possibilities
into the land beyond?

Can life be different than ever
it was thought to be?
Illusions torn away for ever
with the cobwebs of the past?

A new reality calls through the open door
– springbound fresh air blows tantalisingly past
breaking the chains which bind and hold
– to set one stumbling on the grass beyond.
No path, no promises – maybe just a hint of dreams
– an embracing acceptance of new possibilities
– the knowledge finally glimpsed and held.
A new day is beckoning – a new day can be.

It was a cold November evening. I stood alone outside the College of Further Education, clutching my papers in my hand – and shaking with fear! It was ten months since my husband had left me. Apart from going to church services and events, this was the first thing I had done alone since then. Only I hadn't done it yet! I had booked for a six-week course on making wired flowers in icing to decorate Christmas cakes. I wanted to do it, but I felt paralysed with fear. Afterwards, when I tried to analyse why I had felt like this, I realised that I felt as though everyone in the class that night would know that my husband had left me for another woman. I felt ashamed, and vulnerable. I don't quite know how I expected them to have that knowledge as we were all strangers! And I could not even remember the tutor's name! At that stage, I still wore my wedding ring on my left hand, so I imagine the very worst they could have thought of me was that I was rather nervous!

But used as I was to warm, friendly church groups (well, most of the time anyway!), I found the whole thing disconcertingly impersonal. Some of the class as it turned out, already knew each other, but there were those of us who had never seen each other before. With hindsight, I think that was a good thing for it gave me the chance to try out my water wings in water that wasn't too deep, or too suffocatingly warm. I finished the course. I enjoyed the classes. I learnt how to make wired flowers in icing. But as it got a tiny bit easier to go each week, I realised I was beginning to believe there is life beyond marriage breakdown. I remember, after that first night, feeling inordinately brave as I left college with the others, walked back to *my* car, to drive back to *my* flat; I mentally patted myself on the back!

'Peeping out' after being left on your own can be excruciatingly painful and difficult. Some people can't face it and are unable to go out properly or relate to other people. I believe we have to try and get the balance right. After I had learnt to cope with going out, I went a bit 'over the top' and friends and family alike left messages on my answerphone complaining that I was never in – actually, if I'm honest, they still do! We can, of course, 'run away' from our pain, but if we face up to it and get the balance right about going out and socialising, that frees us to learn how to convert our times alone, from loneliness into aloneness. Sure, there will always be times, if we stay on our own, when we will be lonely – we wouldn't be human if there weren't.

I found that we have to get to know ourselves first, as individual people – as opposed to knowing ourselves as the wife/husband of so and so.

After that, we need to learn to respect ourselves enough to meet our own needs.

Then we need to look at our budget and see the areas in which we would like to develop socially. And every so often we need to reassess the situation. I would like to look at these three points one by one. But before I do that, I would like to give a little word of warning about one aspect of 'going it alone' which I learnt the hard way.

Of course, as we begin to try out our new solo social wings, we shall make mistakes – we wouldn't be human if we didn't! Don't try and run, before you can walk. I made that mistake. As I have mentioned before, I absolutely adore ballet, and most forms of dance. A few months after my husband had left me, in the town where I now live, a ballet company came to the theatre and I decided there was no way I could miss it. I had only seen the notice a few days before the performance, so as there was not time to arrange to go with anyone, I decided to go alone. I thought, rather naively, that my great love of dance would overcome any nervous scruples about being alone. After work, I washed my hair and 'put my face on' very carefully – not the usual three minute slap on foundation and play around with eye makeup and lipstick! I chose a silk blouse and a rather classy black skirt which is my favourite, and in which I feel good. I felt I looked at least OK and that I wouldn't stand out in a crowd. I checked I had the ticket I had luckily managed to get despite being so late booking, and set out for the theatre. I parked my car, walked the short distance to the theatre, and went inside. So far, so good. Then I decided I would order an interval drink, so feeling very brave, I ordered a gin and tonic, 'with ice and a slice', to be ready in the first interval. So far, still OK. I found my seat, and began to feel quite at home as in front of me was a lady from my church – another 'ballet buff' – and we chatted about ballet in general and the programme that evening. The ballet was not the best I had ever seen, but I enjoyed it, especially the second dance, which was a very beautiful duet to a haunting melody. So, thus renewed, I went to the bar to collect my drink. It was then that I began to feel a little awkward, because everyone else seemed to be either in couples, or in groups, so I edged my way to the back of the crowd, and stood against the wall, trying to look as inconspicuous as possible. The G and T was good, and I sipped away until I suddenly felt someone's eyes on me. I looked up, and saw a woman watching me with such an open look of pity and compassion on her face, that I felt myself go scarlet. I gulped down the remaining drink in one, and rushed out to the loo, where in the privacy of the small compartment, I tried to recover my composure – and tried to stop my head reeling from drinking spirits that fast!

That woman – and I did not recognise her at all – may just as well have been screaming, 'Look at this girl in the corner everybody, she's on her own.' She was, in fact, probably an extremely nice person who was both sensitive and insightful, but her look completely floored me.

I think from that I learnt that the next time I would either stay in my seat, or make sure I didn't go to the ballet alone. Actually I have been many times since that first time, and have always gone in company – one of the bonuses of new friends and a new social circle. I suppose we don't really know what we can do unless we try, but that evening taught me that however well *I* think I'm doing, more shows in my face than I'd like people to see, so I have learnt not to expect too much from myself too soon.

If someone is in a wheelchair, or using crutches because of a broken leg, everyone can see what the problem is. They can't walk unaided. But we don't put broken hearts in wheelchairs, and the crutches we use are invisible. We wouldn't go up to a person who had broken his leg two weeks previously and say, 'Ah well, Jim, let me see, you've had your leg in plaster for two weeks now. I know you broke it in three places, but I think we'll take the plaster off, and you can start bearing weight on it again!' Ridiculous, isn't it? But it's equally ridiculous to say to a person whose spouse has recently left them, 'Ah well, Jane, your husband left three weeks ago now, so I think it's time you started socialising again and getting out, and bearing responsibility for these church events!' We have to learn not to expect too much of ourselves, and not to let other people put false expectations on to us either.

Now to go on the the three points I spoke of earlier.

Know Yourself
Learning to know ourselves as individuals and not as someone's husband or wife is at first very difficult. When we are first on our own it is difficult for us, and for those who knew us before, to relate to us as a single person. This is especially true if our spouse had a leading role in the community. I was used to always being introduced as 'the vicar's wife' – a term I disliked, because it took away from my identity every time it was used. I was proud to be both my husband's wife, and the wife of the vicar. But people found it simply

201

impossible to say, 'John, this is Sue, she leads sacred dance in our church,' or 'she is a nurse/cook', or whatever I was doing at the time. I got used to it, even though sometimes I was tempted to reply, 'And this person introducing me is the electrician's, butcher's or solicitor's wife'!

Of course, for each of us it will be different, because we all had differing levels of dependence on our spouses. For example, my husband always managed all the finances, because I seem to get in a muddle with figures. I knew nothing about tax forms, car licence forms, council tax form or all the other myriad forms there are, which it seems are necessary just to live! I had to learn, and I had to learn fast. I made loads of mistakes, but that was mostly the way I learnt! When we were still together, my husband used to say to me, 'I don't know how you'd ever manage on your own. You'd be in jail within weeks!' Well, I am very happy to have proved him wrong! Not only am I not in jail, I've never been 'in the red', although at times it has been most incredibly difficult. It has taken all this time to lose my fear of official forms. True, sometimes when one comes, my heart beats a little faster and I begin to feel the panic rising, but most of the time I put them on the table and think, 'Oh, what the heck . . . !'

It is only with time, and as we develop new interests and new areas of our lives, that those of us who have been very dependent on our spouses, learn to develop fully, and formulate our own opinion about things. Many times in the early days, I had to stop myself trotting out 'the party line' that I'd heard my husband use. As I gained a little in self confidence, I became less afraid to express what I thought about things – I got less convinced that what I thought was wrong because it wasn't the same as my husband.

We have to learn to listen to our own inner voice, which, if we only give it the space, will dictate our own needs to us clearly and honestly. I write this so much to

myself, having recently ignored this voice and consequently having suffered from 'nervous and physical
exhaustion'. I ignored what my body was saying to me
and pushed myself, for week after week. I used to wake
up completely exhausted, after sleeping very badly. I
forced myself to go to work each day. More than one of
the nuns in the convent where I worked, had repeatedly said to me, 'I wish you could get some rest, you
look awfully tired.' And I, in my stupidity had replied,
'Oh well, it's nothing that two weeks uninterrupted
sleep won't cure!' and had then carried on pushing
myself!

So through all this, I have had to learn the very hard
lesson, that what *I* think is as valid as what anyone else
thinks. I had a terrible identity crisis the first time my
husband left me, and another one the second time he
left. But I now see very clearly that there are parts of
my personality which have developed and blossomed,
which would have had to lie dormant if we had stayed
together. And now, although I wish with all my heart
we could have stayed together, I am beginning to think
that I am glad to have had the chance to develop these.
I know there will be others who will know what I mean
when I say I am finding exciting areas of myself I did
not know existed. It's exciting – if a little scary at times!
If you are in the middle of your own identity crisis all I
can say is: 'Hang in there; give yourself time; go for
counselling if you can; let your friends help you, listen
to them when they tell you of your strengths and weaknesses.' And perhaps most important of all, 'Don't be
afraid of the new you that develops. When you get to
know yourself better, you may well have some pleasant surprises. But whatever you do, *don't hurry the process*. Let it happen naturally.' And remember, God
made us, and He wants us all to develop our full poten-
tial, so He will help us do this, both in terms of discovery and self acceptance.

Learn to Respect Yourself

Point number two is learning to respect ourselves enough to meet our own needs. I have touched a little on this in my first point in the way we must not push ourselves too hard. But there is much more involved than that.

Since doing the Myers-Briggs course, it has been a great help to me to know that I gain inner strength from being alone. The personality typing is done through answering a 'multi-choice' questionnaire, then being assessed and lectured by a trained tutor. It helps both in terms of understanding yourself, and others. It also helps in relationships with other people, being a useful tool in realising why we and others, say or think certain things. To use a popular phrase, it helps to know where we are 'coming from'! Several conference centres run this course, and although it is not specifically Christian in content, it can be used in a very creative way to help us develop in our Christian lives. It has 'given me permission' to know and accept all sorts of things about myself. With self knowledge, comes self awareness and acceptance of our needs. I have had to learn to say 'no' when people ask me to do things that I know are either too much, or I haven't the time. For those of us who have to work full time, it is a constant balancing act to fit in all the other things that life demands, or that we want to do. If we run our own homes, then there is all that that entails – shopping, cleaning, washing, ironing and a host of other things before we even start to think about what we actually *want* to do! It can get to feel that life is a constant struggle against time. That was what happened to me when I was ill with exhaustion. What I *should* have done was to slow down, assess my life a little, gone to my doctor earlier and been more honest with him about how awful I felt, instead of being afraid of 'making a fuss'. If we do have to juggle our lives like this, then we must make sure and leave enough space and time for us.

And we must do that with pride – not apology. I have found that when I have had to pull out of things, the world actually had the effrontery to keep on spinning, and life as we know it, did not stop!

We may well find on our voyage of discovery, that we have to respect ourselves enough to realise we need new ways of worshipping God. For some, their experiences may lead them to develop the more contemplative side of their natures, whilst others may need a freer, more charismatic approach to God. Some people may want to give formal church a miss for a while. The lesson I had to learn was that if I felt strongly about something, then I had to listen to what I was saying to myself. In the early days, I had to miss corporate worship in church for several weeks together.

One practice I developed, which I do to this day, is that on my birthday and at Christmas, I buy myself a present. I remember that first Christmas, my daughters were amused and pleased to find under the Christmas tree, a little parcel with 'To me, from me, because I care about you' written on it!

If we can develop fully the person God wants us to be, and that our new circumstances allow us to be, the next thing we have to do in terms of respecting ourselves, is to learn to love ourselves. I can almost hear the corporate indrawn breaths of any counsellors who may be reading this book! I can hear them saying, 'Well, this should be good – I wonder what she's going to say now!' Well, the simple truth is, this is the point I have reached now so I can actually say very little! I can share with you my confusion in knowing just how very much God loves me, and yet being fully aware of that, *I* have great difficulty in loving myself. I don't want to insult God, and say in effect, 'I know You've made me, but I'm sorry, I don't like Your handiwork.' All I can do is to tell Him I *do* know how much He loves me, and that has been the only thing which has kept me going at times, go on to thank Him for that, and ask Him to help me to love His child – me. I know He understands this, because He understands everything about all of us, and I must rest in that knowledge while I work on my problems, both with help and in the privacy of my communion with Him. And I must listen to, and accept, what my friends tell me about the person I am.

Developing a social life

My third point is looking at areas in which we would like to develop socially. The first thing I want to say about this, is that developing a social life does *not* have to cost a lot of money. There will be those who look at this and say, 'Well, it's all right for *her*, I can't afford it!' Well, it's not all right for me, and neither can I! I share your financial struggles, and as I have said before in this book, those who talk glibly about 'living by faith' – usually from positions of financial security – really should try it for a good length of time. It's OK for a week or two, but several years on, I find it relentlessly exhausting. True, God does lovely things, and He *does* supply our needs, but often He takes us to the limit first – and on bad days, it feels like beyond that limit. So, let's look at ways we can develop socially within our budget.

It is a good idea to make a list of our interests, then cross off the ones which are being addressed at the present time. Then looking at what is left, make a list of the ones you want to develop. Obviously on a tight income, it's no good writing down something like 'Llama farming in Peru'! The list has to be realistic. Then make a list of the time you have available. When I took my six-week course in wired flower making, I had to ensure that I was free for six weeks on Monday nights. Taking any form of further education involves a certain cost and time commitment. I love to learn new things and to develop existing knowledge, but I find the cost of evening classes prohibitive. However there are often grants available, or family or friends who will help to pay for them as a Christmas or birthday gift. When I wanted to do my class, I opened a Post Office account to save up the necessary fees. It gave me a great feeling of satisfaction when the amount needed was reached!

One of the things on my list was table tennis. So, with another friend who loves to play, I joined a local table tennis club. Along with some others, we formed a team, and this year will be our third season playing league matches. We're not brilliant, but we thoroughly enjoy both our practices and our match nights. It's relatively cheap, and we meet all sorts of new people – sometimes all going for a drink after our matches. We have enormous fun, and our excitement is phenomenal if we actually win a game! I have become much closer friends with the person I play with, and for both of us it's especially good, as it is not something connected with our church. We need to get the balance right about this. It's no good being 'so heavenly minded, we're of no earthly use'! For those who like sport, swimming is another inexpensive way of relaxing and getting exercise. For around two pounds, and in just over half an hour, I swim thirty-two lengths, which is the equivalent of a major workout, and as far as I am concerned, much more enjoyable! It's quick, easy and cheap – provided we can swim of course, and if not, we're never too old to learn?! But for those who definitely are not swimmers, walking is free, and a very good thing to do with a friend. But I've already shared earlier my own opinions about that particular pastime!

We may well find that as we develop as people after the trauma of separation or divorce, new areas of ministry open up for us. For instance, I am much freer now to develop my own ministry of sacred dance, both in terms of dancing myself, and in teaching it. I doubt very much if my writing would have developed in the way it has, if I had not been on my own. There will be areas in which you will want to develop in this way. If you're unsure about your gifts, and yet have time to give to the church, talk it over with your vicar, priest, or minister. I am *quite* sure they will find some way in which you can help the church! It may be visiting folk who can't get out of their homes. It may be being a sidesperson, or leading a home group, or being on the ministry team to pray with people. *Whatever* you do, it can be used, from washing up to preaching sermons. If we have indeed learnt to accept ourselves – or at least, started to – then we shall also be learning to accept the gifts God has given us, and offering them back to Him.

Another way we may want to develop socially, is in the area of new relationships with members of the opposite sex. There are many Christian dating agencies, or friendship fellowships. I myself have just tentatively joined one. I felt I had to fill in the forms and send them off, as my daughters were threatening to do it for me, and goodness only knows what *they* would have written! I found a list of these agencies when reading a copy of *Woman Alive*, a magazine 'for today's Christian woman'. I know of some Christians who join secular dating agencies, and that is fine if that is what you want to do. Then there are various groups, some church related, for those who have been through separation or divorce. All these are ways of meeting new people, of expanding our horizons – of not becoming dull and boring.

I enjoy eating out with friends, but as this can be expensive, I have joined forces with a girl friend, and we are busy drawing up a 'star rating' of all the pubs within a fifty-mile radius. Of course we consider it our public duty to do this, in case anyone ever asks our advice on the matter! But that's not so expensive, and in the pursuit of our 'public duty', we have some very good meals and a good natter into the bargain!

I do think though that everyone, however tight their budget, should have one extravagance. Obviously we can't be overdrawn and silly about this, but most of us can do a spot of overtime to fund the occasional 'treat'. We all have one thing about which we are passionate. Mine, of course, is ballet. Now *that* is expensive – although there are moves afoot to bring it down to a more realistic price for the general public, and not just the chosen few. So I save, or if it's near a birthday, ask for help that way. I suppose for me, going to the ballet touches on respecting myself enough as a person to meet my own needs. I don't just *want* ballet and dance – I need it too. It feeds my soul in a way nothing else can. So pamper yourself from time to time. And again, do it with pride, not apology. Above all – ENJOY! Maybe we should put 'government health warnings' on our treats! 'No feelings of guilt allowed – no worrying about the bank balance. To enjoy to the full, relax, and have a really good time!'

When I asked my helpers with this book about how they developed their social lives after being left, their answers varied tremendously.

Christine replied simply, 'I do not go out socially and I do not belong to a church.'

At the other end of the spectrum, Robert replied, 'I carried on as before. I was trapped by the expectations around me. As well as the parochial social life – which is not extensive – it was not easy turning up on my own to other social events, when until then I had done things as part of a couple. I learnt that people are very good on the whole. Once people knew that my wife was not with me and word got around what the situation was, it was OK. Not nice really, and not like it ought to be, or indeed anything like as enjoyable as it once was. Social events invariably bring a shadow with them, even now. The unaccompanied male of middle years is a pretty forlorn sight, even if he is well dressed! I don't think in terms of "easy or difficult" – much more in terms of "duty". I have got used to it now.

'Sometimes being asked to make up numbers at a social event can be challenging, especially when the hostess feels an introduction to the other single lady present is a helpful thing to do for you! That is life, and drinks are welcome in that situation! Other events where there is a predominance of married people can make you feel rather lonesome, despite the warmth of friendship. I have every sympathy with "the singles' brigade". It is not comfortable. Thankfully social life for me is only a small part of my life.

'Shortly after separation, I felt it was important to fix up a "date". I invited a lady out to lunch. It was an extremely hard thing to do, after twenty-five years of not doing that sort of thing – of always sharing company. To do so was very hard. I had to break through the barrier of being single again. It was very nerve racking, I felt stupid and unsure of myself, and angry at having to do such a thing.

'Yet I knew it was something I had to do in order to regain my selfhood, and to survive as a human being after separation. In the event it was an excellent lunch and very pleasant. I went home realising I could be single again. It was strange however – I realised there was no disloyalty involved, and I had discovered an unaccustomed area of personal freedom.'

In the middle of these two 'poles' is Brenda who says, 'I started going out quite quickly as I needed something to fill my mind in order to get through the days. Also, I found I needed the support of my friends and family, and the only way to get that was to go and find it. No one wants to visit a miserable bitter woman. It was not easy, especially as the events were mainly things we had been to together. It is getting easier as time goes on. Also, I find it difficult as I realise I am a little afraid of being hurt again, so new relationships are approached with caution.'

Elizabeth has much younger children – all three were under four when her husband left her. At the end of the first month she took her eldest son to a Latin American evening. It was her first outing as a single parent. She says she felt 'very odd, because I was acutely aware there were lots of families there.' She feels that although she does not use her children to hide behind, they do give her a certain security when she is out. She occasionally goes out with three girl friends for a drink. 'That feels safe to me', she says of these outings.

Two years after being left, she went to a party given by an old college friend, where there were lots of unattached people. Elizabeth says, 'I found conversation difficult as I didn't know any of them – and I had promised myself not to talk about my children.'

At this stage she is not really interested in meeting someone else, as her children are her chief concern. She says she would love to meet 'a loving and caring man who could be a father to my children.' But as they are so young she is concentrating on giving them a happy and stable home, and family life. She adds, 'But I have got a brain and I do feel ready for some adult conversation!'

Because she did need to meet other people, and not just be with tiny children all day, she took her youngest children to a play group where she stayed to help, and enjoyed meeting the other mothers very much. Elizabeth also attended an 'Alpha' course at her church, which she also enjoyed. It was a mixture of social and spiritual, as the evening always started with a meal. But it wasn't until the last evening that she felt able to share a little of her story with the rest of the group.

It is clear from my experiences and those of my friends, that 'peeping out' will be different for each one, depending on so many factors. The vast majority of us do not decide to become hermits, so sooner or later we try out our new social wings. And here I would reiterate several things. Give yourself TIME. Time to get to know yourself. After all, if *you* don't really know yourself, how can you expect others to know you? Time also, to learn to respect yourself enough to meet your own needs. Then, when you feel ready – not when well meaning friends tell you that you're ready – you can start to 'put your toe in the water'. Don't attempt too much too soon. Don't be thrown if you get set backs – like my first night at the ballet! Treat yourself kindly, and with respect. You have, after all, the rest of your life to develop new social skills!

And most important of all, remember that actually you are not really on your own. You journey with a Man who is infinitely kind, and who understands you better than you understand yourself. He does not push you too hard. If you listen carefully, you will hear Him say to you, 'Well done my child, well done. And remember, I am with you always, wherever you go.'

Peeping Out

I'm peeping out Lord – peeping out.
Learning to live again –
Only a tiny bit at a time –
But I'm peeping out Father; looking round corners.
And every time I look
I see two arms reaching out to hold me
– I see You.
I'm going out and doing things Lord.
I often feel afraid –
But I pluck up courage and go.
I'm peeping out – pushing new doors.
And whenever I do that
Always, on the other side of the door
– I find You.

Some days, I simply can't do it Lord
– It's just too much.
Don't want to relate to others at all –
But it's then Lord, that You peep in at me

212

–I only have to raise my head
And You hug me and hold me close.
You are there.
I'm learning to live a new life Lord –
You are teaching me how.
Sometimes it's trial and error, taste and see.
But I'm peeping out – trying hard.
And when I do
You're always there to encourage and love me
– You never fail.

I'm peeping out Lord – peeping out
Learning to live again
Learning to love
To trust
Not to be afraid Lord
I'm peeping out, with You holding my hand
And everywhere I look, and everywhere I go
– I see You.

Chapter Fifteen

REALITY – AN UNSHAKEABLE GOD

Heartbeats
Two heartbeats.
One loud, tangible and within,
One distant, misty – and within.
One heard constantly, every day –
One heard fleetingly – just for moments of time.
Two heartbeats Lord –
Yours – and mine.

One you cannot escape.
Lub, dup – lub, dup – lub, dup.
One you don't want to escape –
Love, peace – love, peace – love, peace.
Can they ever touch – can they?
Two heartbeats Lord –
Yours – and mine.

Mine I can only see on a monitor.
Yours Lord I see in moonlight – in a smile.
I see it too in others' suffering, and their pain.
I see it in the morning sky – I hear it in the wind.
Is it possible that they could touch?
Two heartbeats Lord –
Yours – and mine.

Let me join with you Lord – let me.
My heart is open, longing for You.
Reach out from the Cross, reach out.

And with Your pain, touch my heart with Yours.
I long – I breathe – You hear – You breathe.
One heartbeat Lord –
Yours – and mine.

'My child, do not choose "not to be",
for before the stars were put in place
I had conceived you in my heart;
and I hold you in my arms for all time;
you are carried forever within my love.'

I was going from my bathroom into my lounge when it happened. As I walked through the hall, I was quite suddenly completely overwhelmed by a feeling and knowledge of God's love for me. It totally immersed me. It was wonderful – warm and comforting – like being hugged and protected all at the same time! Afterwards I described it to a friend as being 'splattered' against a wall! It only lasted a few seconds, and yet it felt like a lifetime. I walked into the lounge in a kind of daze and sat down. I always have a notepad and pen ready on my table in case I feel a poem 'coming on', or as I frequently call it, rumbling round in my head! I used to call it rumbling round in my brain, but if I did that and my daughters were at home, one of them would look at me in a rather pitying way and say, 'Your what, Mum . . . ?!'

I reached for the pad and started to write. As I wrote I felt a sense of excitement – I felt something special was happening. I remember the phone rang while I was writing. The noise distracted me, so I answered it. It was my sister. I said, 'Sorry, can't stop now – mid poem!', and put the phone down! My sister is one of my greatest encouragers in my writing, so I knew she understood. I continued with my 'scribbling'. Suddenly I knew it was finished.

As I read the poem through, I realised that tears of joy, sadness and laughter – all together – were stream-

ing down my face. I rushed round to my close friend
Linda, and rather excitedly showed her the poem
telling her how it had come. She was just as excited as
I was, and said it was a poem that had to be shared
with our church. In fact, it has been taken and shared
much further afield than that. Not only has it been
shared with our church, it has been sent out to
Rwanda, to be read to church leaders there, and it has
been sent to Cyprus and Pakistan. It has been taken
home by hundreds of women as I have spoken at different meetings. It was thrilling to be a part of it, and
even now when I read it, it speaks to me anew. I share
it with you now. Gentlemen, even though it was origi-
nally written for a 'daughter', please substitute 'son', as
it is for everyone.

Lovesong

How precious you are my daughter to me –
How precious you are to me.

When the past reaches out to haunt you, I will hold
you close –
And when the future frightens you, I will calm your
fears –
I will be with you in every waking moment, in every
sleeping dream –
I will heal you when you are feeling broken –
I will wipe your tears when you are weeping –
I will hold your hand when the wind blows hard –
I will cherish you when you feel unloved –
I will be beside you when you are rejected –
I will light the path when the way seems dark –
I will give you hope when you are frightened –
And when you feel abandoned, I will come and be
your love.
I will be your light when your world is all in darkness –
I will suffer with you when you are in pain –

*I will hear what you are saying when you feel
misunderstood –
I will close my arms around you when you need to
be protected –
When the world sounds harsh, you will hear my
gentle sigh –
And when you feel you are alone, tenderly I will
speak your name.*

*I will gently lift your head when the way seems
heavy –
I will watch beside you when you are feeling weary –
I will be within your sleep when you are dreaming –
I will help you stand when you awake –
I will help you live when you feel like dying –
And when you are despairing, I will come and kiss
your head.*

*I will keep you trusting when you are afraid –
I will keep you faithful when others do not know me –
I will keep you safe when all around is dangerous –
I will keep you weak, for then you will be strong –
I will keep you mine through all eternity –
I will love you always with a never-ending love –
When you turn to look at me, I will touch you with
my hand –
And with my eternal tenderness, you will hear me
whisper.*

*Oh, how precious you are my daughter to me –
How precious you are to me.*

I have explained at length about how this poem was
written, because to me, it is a constant reminder of
God's love for us. I have at various times experienced
every line of 'Lovesong'. On some days now, when
things feel very black, one line will leap out at me; it
will wrap itself around me, just as God did in my hall

217

on the day the poem was given to me. Isaiah 43, verses 4b and 5, says, '. . . because you are precious to me and because I love you and give you honour. Do not be afraid – I am with you!' A verse which I have always loved. That day in my hall, Almighty God paused a little, and reached down and touched me. Sin filled, stumbling, sometimes lost, me – but He still touched me with His absolutely unshakeable love.

In my Christian journey with God I have found over the years that He sometimes gives these experiences of being 'lifted up' at unexpected times and in unexpected places. Then later, as with 'Lovesong', we can look back at them and take heart. Many times I have read that poem again – not because *I* wrote it, but because God did, and I know that He spoke directly to me when it was given. It does *not* say, 'My beloved daughter, everything is going to be all right. Just praise me even though you are in the pits, and everything will be wonderful. Nothing bad will happen to you, everything will be sweetness and light – you are immune from problems!' On the contrary, it shows us that our Heavenly Father fully understands every feeling that we have, and He is with us in them all. Feelings themselves are neutral – they are not either 'right' or 'wrong'. It is what we *do* with them that matters.

There is a chorus – try as I can, I can't remember it – but whenever it comes up on the overhead projector in a service I refuse to sing it. It actually makes me furious! It says something like, 'If you have Jesus then all your problems disappear.' What rubbish! If we have Jesus, then our problems often seem to *increase*! But of course, the difference is that He is there to help us in them. But that false triumphalist way of looking at things is wrong, and I believe, does a lot of harm to people. They feel guilty because their problems have *not* gone. And they won't just because we are Christians. We are often told to 'give them to the Lord.' But this can be misunderstood. When we give the problem to the Lord, what we are *really* giving to the Lord is our anxiety about our ability to bear it. The Lord does not simply take the problem away. But when we give our anxieties to God He honours that, and He takes that very act of giving, using it to transform some part of us, to enable us to carry the burden of our problems.

A very long time ago, I wrote what I call 'my collect' (I have used it at the beginning of Chapter Two). But heed my warning, it's a dangerous prayer to pray! If you do, anything may happen! One friend who took it away and prayed it from her heart, immediately had her life turned completely upside down! And my own life has not been exactly smooth since I prayed it for the first time! I wrote it when I was sitting in a very old church whilst on holiday when my girls were quite young. As I remember, it was one of the first 'scrib- blings' God gave me. Perhaps with more wisdom at the time, I should have realised by its very content, that there would be rough seas ahead. But I say that now with hindsight – and who among us ever guesses that our whole life is, one day, in the not too distant future, going to be completely smashed by the one person we love most in the world?

Whatever You would ask of me O Lord Christ
– take.
For in the asking
is the giving
– and in the taking
I receive.

When 'giving our problems to the Lord', take for instance, difficulties with finances. I can go to church this Sunday, kneel down and say to God, 'Lord, I give you all my anxieties about money. I don't know if I've enough in the bank to pay my rent and all my other bills this month. I give it to You.' When I leave church and arrive home, the bills are still there, waiting to be paid. And my bank balance is still too small. Now it is certainly true that on occasions God reaches down and in a lovely way inspires some fellow Christian to 'supply another's needs', and there have been many times in the last few years when I have been so thankful for that. But this is what I meant when I spoke in an earlier chapter about those in positions of financial security talking airily about how we must 'live by faith.' Of course I can't deny the truth of God's provision for us – maybe I just lack the necessary faith to live like this all the time. All I know is that there will be those of you who will identify with me when I write the following. When I am tired after a hard day's work; when I have done all I can to meet my commitments; when the car needs a service which I can't afford, but I know I *have* to keep running it to earn a living; when the optician has just written to me saying I need an eye test; when the council tax has just gone up, but my wages haven't; when I have toothache, and need a mortgage to pay the dentist's bill; when the food cupboard is empty; when the TV licence is due; when the phone bill is waiting to be paid, and I have to be back on duty in ten hours' time in an intelligent frame of mind – then I feel pretty fed up!

At those times, I can't simply 'look at God, and my problems disappear'. They don't. And I will be uncompromising in stating that this is not so. If you have people saying this to you, then my heart goes out to you. But DO NOT FEEL GUILTY, because what they are telling you is simply not true. *Of course* you will feel tired, and dejected, and wonder when it will all end. It *is* exhausting – I know, I have lived with it for years. Do not give up, however much you feel like it, because what we *can* do is to look at Him and say, 'Help me Lord, I'm doing all I can and it still isn't enough. I'm tired and near to breaking point. Please help me', and then go on to tell Him exactly how we feel. I believe it is far better to accept the trust in God which we do have, but still be honest about how we feel. God does *not* want us to pretend, or be accused of 'lack of faith' by others. He wants so much for us to be ruthlessly truthful when telling Him how we feel, for when we are completely honest with Him, He takes our openness and uses it as the incense of our offering to Him.

It is not, of course, only finances that will take us to breaking point. It is the constant pain from a broken heart. It is the deep wounds of rejection, grief and loss. It is trying to live with the memory of things that were once ours, which have been ripped away from us. It is remembering a life spent together, which is now gone. For some of us, it is the unique agony of still loving our spouse, and knowing that the love which was once ours, is now being given to someone else. It's thinking about the man/woman we love, living, moving and being, and we cannot be with them. I believe that for all these things, and more, the key factor that will unlock God's love and comfort to us, is honesty. God hates falsity as much as we do, and He only wants to hear us praising Him if we mean it. Not doing it because we feel we *ought* to, because then it doesn't come from the heart. I know some folk put on praise tapes to get them 'in the mood'. For me, that rarely works. I find it better to put on a quiet meditation type tape, which will soothe my soul and stroke my hurts, and help bring me to a place of peace. What we *can* say is, 'Thank You Father, that You love me and understand this place of pain I'm in.' That really does come from our hearts, and God will honour it.

One of the wonderful ways God did supply my needs when I was at a very low ebb, was to provide a new job for me when I felt I had to leave the convent. I started work on the nursing team at Burrswood. Burrswood was founded in 1948 by the late Dorothy Kerrin, who herself received a miraculous healing in 1912. It describes itself as '. . . a unique Christian centre, providing short-term in-patient care. There are two resident doctors, visiting consultants in many specialities and a team of caring nurses. Acute illness can be investigated and treated and expert symptom control offered for chronic and terminal conditions. Skilled counsellors work alongside the doctors, physiotherapists and chaplains.'

It describes its ministry in the following way: 'In our hospital, orthodox medicine combines with Christian prayer and counsel to care for the "whole" person – body, mind, spirit and emotions. Many who come need help in more than one of these areas. The whole community, with their differing gifts, tasks and abilities, work towards this end. In addition to that of our full time chaplains, ministry is offered through teams drawn from laity throughout our community. We offer traditional and sacramental ministry, as well as placing value on informal prayer. Whatever means we use, we believe that we are but channels for the healing love and prayer of Jesus Christ.' It also says that 'This unique Christian centre for healthcare and ministry is located in a beautiful 220 acre estate some 30 miles south of London.' It also happens to be six miles from my flat!

I see the provision of this job, at a time when all the 'chips were down', and my self confidence was in shreds, as a direct gift from God to me. I was the 'vicar's wife' in a large and thriving parish, with an active healing ministry, then I had that wrenched away from me when my husband left. When he returned, I worked for nearly four years at Crowhurst, the Church's Healing Centre in Sussex. Then we moved to a parish which also had a developing healing ministry. My husband and I ministered together while he was a priest there. Then that was snatched away from me when he left again with another woman. I now find myself involved right back in the heart of His ministry of healing at Burrswood! It is a privilege to work there, and I absolutely love it. But I do *not* believe in coincidences, and I think I have gotten hold of the fact that God wants me involved in the healing ministry. I don't fully understand why, but after all that's happened, I accept it. God's purposes will not ultimately be frustrated, and maybe it's not the place I would have been involved in this ministry, or in quite the same way as if my husband had stayed in the priesthood. But God does appear to have been remarkably persistent in placing me back in this ministry. Certainly it is one very close to my heart. My Benedictine name is Sister Luke, and St Luke, the good doctor, is my patron saint. So through it all I can see the hand of God providing, and guiding me, even though some of the ways this has come about have been dreadfully painful.

When we have seemingly insurmountable problems, God does not always change the problem – He changes us. This does not mean that our reaction is necessarily wrong; but we may just be thoroughly worn down with ongoing problems that cause us severe emotional pain. But the fact is, that when we give our hurts to Him – the tiny ones, because they matter to us, and the big ones, because they are huge, then God really *will* use them and help us carry the weight.

Much has been written on the paradox of suffering and joy, and I would not presume to attempt to add to that. What I *would* say is that I now know God in a much deeper and more real way than I did before my life spiralled out of control. In the places of deepest pain, I have found Him already there and waiting for me, and have met Him in a new, and 'raw' way.

I see it sometimes as if I am a deeply wounded person, lying on the floor. I am covered in wounds and sore places, and if anyone else were to touch me I would scream in agony, and they would add to my pain, even if they were dressing my wounds and helping me to heal. But when God touches me, He dresses my wounds in a different way. He strokes them. I can feel and see Him gently running His own wounded hands over the places in my body and spirit which cause such pain. Yes, sometimes that touch does make me scream at first, but then He tells me to breathe in time with Him – slowly, deeply, thoughtfully, and as we breathe together, He and I, the pain becomes shared, and just about bearable.

A Strange Forgotten Feeling

'Lord, what is it stirring in my heart?
A strange forgotten feeling from long ago?
It feels like rays of sunshine, but on the inside –
Quite suddenly the world looks different
The sky has never seemed so blue
The sun somehow feels even warmer than before
– What is it Lord, stirring in my heart?
A strange forgotten feeling from long ago?

It's like a distant hazy memory
And it makes me feel like a child again
I want to reach out, hold it, and keep it –
I don't ever want it to escape
It makes me feel like running through the grass
– Like jumping in the fields and picking buttercups
What is it Lord, stirring in my heart?
That strange forgotten feeling from long ago?

Nothing has changed in my life.
It's still a really hard and difficult place to be
I still get tired and wonder if I can make it
I still need You to help me through every second
– All the problems are still the same as yesterday.
So what is it Lord, stirring in my heart?
That strange forgotten feeling from long ago?
Why can I feel it Lord – for nothing has changed?'

'No, my child – you are wrong.
Something has changed –

> *You have – you've changed*
> *You let me strip away more and more of your*
> *defences*
> *You have let me into the centre of your heart –*
> *When you opened the door of your soul to me*
> *I came in and sat down with you and ate –*
> *You opened your heart to me and gave me yourself*
> *And in that giving my child, my beloved one*
> *I took you, I took you to myself.*
>
> *For I can change the darkest night into the*
> *rainbow's end*
> *I can lift the thickest fog and change it into sunshine*
>
> *I am there in the deepest places to lift you up*
> *I can transform every hurt and use it for myself.*
>
> *Nothing has changed my child*
> *But yet everything has changed*
> *For you gave the difficult hurting parts of your life*
> *to me*
> *Now I hold them, and you in the palm of my hand*
> *And see child – my scars fit your pain so perfectly.*
>
> *That strange forgotten feeling stirring in your heart*
> *It's me child – some people call it happiness*
> *But I can tell you my child, my beloved one,*
> *It's me – it's me – it's me.'*

The experiences of marriage breakdown and divorce raise unique questions for Christians. They are experiences which *will* change us. To suffer that much pain and remain the same, is not possible. I asked my four contributors how they felt they had changed. This is what they said.

Christine said simply: 'Yes, of course I've changed. How can one go through suffering and not change?'

Brenda said: 'Yes, I've changed. I am a different person now. I no longer feel that I have to live up to the expectations of others. I can be who I am in the full knowledge that Jesus loves me. I also have far more compassion and a heart for those who hurt. I weep more easily and watch my tongue a lot more, remembering that God gave me two ears and only one mouth!'

Elizabeth said: 'I've got to know myself better. I now acknowledge not only my weaknesses, but also my strengths. I'm proud of who and what I am, and I'm proud of my family. I now have proud principles that are central to my life, and through all the distress and pain I'm discovering a calm centre in myself of which I keep hold.

'My identity was very much as mother and wife, and it was difficult to see myself as a single parent.

'This doesn't mean I find life easy. My life can be very stressful. Certain events and people can knock my self esteem and I can then question my ability to cope – but in spite of this my self esteem is growing. I'm now much stronger, more independent. I have to say I'm more cautious of new people I meet.'

Robert said in answer to my question: 'I suppose the inner person is always the same. I am aware that I am on a journey through life, and circumstances are bound to change. The loss of my marriage is a pretty severe change of course, but it is part of my journey, and I don't think I could have avoided it, sad to say, so I press on. The process has deepened my understanding of life and myself a great deal. The fundamentals of my life remain constant inasmuch as I can understand them, and the continuity of my life seems to be as much on stream as ever.'

Lastly, I asked my friends this question: 'Do you have any examples of God showing you His love and faithfulness through all this?'

Christine answered: 'No, but I know that God waits patiently for me to turn back to Him.'

Brenda said: 'The one story (among many) I would like to relate was when I was feeling a lot better (after a period of two years), when my husband rang to ask when the decree absolute was coming through, "Because I want to get married on Saturday." I just fell to pieces. I railed at God. I shouted and bawled; fortunately I live in a detached house! I was livid that God was not answering my prayers and bringing my husband back to me. After I had used all my energy, and quietened down, I asked Him to give me a passage of Scripture. I opened my Bible at random, and "For your Maker is your husband – the LORD Almighty is his name – the Holy One of Israel is your Redeemer; he is called the God of all the earth" '(Isaiah 54:5).

'I read on to, and included verse ten – ' "The mountains and hills may crumble, but my love for you will never end; I will keep for ever my promise of peace." So says the Lord who loves you.' – and then spent the rest of the night in prayer. This passage has sustained and upheld me ever since. I knew then that there is a true God, and that He loves and cares about me, and in spite of all the pain, He wants what is best for me.'

And Robert said: 'Yes, there were a number of signs and thoughts and spiritual experiences which paved my road. They have all been most helpful. Prayers have been answered. Grace given, encouragement, endurance and insight. It really has, for me, to be a plentiful experience of God. The truth that I can witness to, is simply that God will share your life with you. All of it, suffering, and joy. Perhaps to close, I give you a lovely little story.

'I was very down and in much inner pain at one time. I was doing my duty in bringing the sacrament to an elderly housebound person. It was a very sweet and personal occasion. Our Lord was silently present. The Communion had been received, and we shared a deep pool of loving silence. In this timeless moment, the Lord said to me, quite clearly: "Robert, your pains are my pains, and my pains are yours." That's all. It was so simple, so sweet and truthful. It was deep consolation given, when most needed. Breathtakingly beautiful. But that is how God is – simple, straightforward, and immensely tender and loving.

'I cannot conceive how I would have survived without God. It would have been impossible. But to have done so, is an enriching experience. That being the case, I am glad to share what I have found with others.'

I know that God has changed me. I echo the thoughts of my four friends. I listen much more now, and say less. I feel I have a much greater depth of empathy and compassion with those who are beaten down by life, and hurting. And of course, I feel that my relationship with God has 'gone up a gear.'

I would like to add here, something I wrote while on a recent holiday. I was with my sister and her family on a boating holiday. It was immediately following the trauma of leaving the convent where I worked. I felt a very real grief for the nuns there, and those on the staff who were my friends. I was recovering from my illness – exhaustion – and was feeling pretty fragile. Day after day had been gloriously hot and sunny, and after taking my turn struggling with heavy lock gates, and the mysteries of 'slackers' and 'clove hitches', I had sat for hours just drinking in the peace of the lovely countryside through which we had travelled. In the heat and peace, there was suddenly one of those timeless moments when earth and heaven meet – and God is there. I had had the following experience only once or twice before, and each time it had taken me hours to 'come down' from the place to which God had lifted me. I grabbed my ever present notepad, and began to write. My family and close friends know me well enough to realise that if I am sitting scribbling furiously over my pad, then it's best to leave me alone – they have a strong instinct for self survival! What I wrote of my experience on that hot summer's day was this.

'I yearn; I long; I reach inwards; I reach outwards; my heart strains ever upwards; my spirit aches, and my whole being cries out for You, O Lord – for You, and You, and You.

I can see You in the beauty of the sun dancing on dappled water – in every ripple, You sing my Lord – from every path You beckon me, my Love – in the breeze on the water, You sing to me my Beloved. Your arms reach out to me, and my heart sings in reply: "My Love, my Life, come – take me to Yourself. Ravish me and do with me as You will."

Whatever is happening here is nothing compared with this joy, this wonder, this indescribable happiness of knowing You – and being known intimately, and passionately, by You. Every day, the wonder is new – is ageless. You call me to Yourself and love me with tenderness and compassion, meeting all my needs; stroking my hurts; soothing my grief; holding me in Your arms – heart to heart, soul mingling with soul – each heartbeat resounding together, for a moment, in unison.

Then after the joining, the ecstasy, I am released – but with reluctance – and then I fall back into Your arms – just nestling, cheek to cheek, in warm, tender, life giving love. It is more gentle than the clouds – yet stronger than the wind – caressing, lingering, touching the senses, till, the spirit having soared, sinks gently to Your feet, where Your scarred hands slowly lift my head – to place a kiss of the purest, most tender love the world has ever known, upon my lips.

And thus reborn, renewed, the kiss becomes Your praises, rising in an ever increasing love song of wonder, joy and thankfulness. Oh my heart, my Beloved One, release me, for my soul is filled, and

until the next time when You take me to Yourself,
I will sing a new song. I will live only to worship
You; I will breathe only to praise You; and I will
move only to dance, and dance, and dance – for
You. For life is a dance – a love dance to You – my
Lover – my Life – my Lord – my JESUS.'

But of course, we cannot always be on this plane. These
are special experiences – rare moments of unexpected
joy and closeness.

On some days God's presence is felt only in the
heartfelt cry of 'Why?' from a life filled with pain. But
the very fact that this is not a meaningless, rhetorical
question, but one which demands an answer, presup-
poses that God is actually there to hear the question in
the first place. His answer may well be the ability to
live with the question, but the important thing is that
we ask it at all.

One cliché we often see written on little cards, and
decorated nicely with squiggles and flowers, is: 'Let go,
and let God'. This is best said to oneself, more than to
other people! But in its stark simplicity, is a great truth.
On those days, and at those times, when our whole
being is filled with pain and grief, all we *can* do is to let
go. Then, and only then, do we allow God to do all the
holding. If we hold on to something – or someone –
then we do not give the full weight of our burden to
Him, so He cannot hold it (or us) in its entirety and its
heartfelt enormity.

The Christian journey never ends. It starts before we
were born, in the heart of God, when He knew us
before we were even formed, as it says in Psalm 139. I
love the Psalms, but that is my favourite, because it
speaks of God's intimate knowledge of each one of us.
In verse 16, it says: 'The days allotted to me had all
been recorded in your book, before any of them ever
began.' I find that a source of immeasurable comfort.
That on the day my mother first held me in her arms,

and looked down on that tiny, helpless baby, God looked down on us both – and knew. He knew that one day in the future, I would meet my husband. He knew that one day I would lose my firstborn son before he was fully formed – but then He knew also that my two healthy, beautiful daughters would be born. He knew that 'the days allotted' to my first baby were not enough, and *I* know that He holds that tiny child in His arms for all time. He knew that one day, I would marry the man I love – and that that love would be thrown back in my face, not once, but three times. And He knew that I would go to places of suffering that some people cannot even imagine, and far more cannot begin to understand. But He also knew that He would make Himself known to me from the first day of my life – that I would never know a day when I did not know Him. And He knew too, that He will always be there for me – that He will always hold me. For however dark the night, He is there in the darkness – and He comes anew with the dawn. He knew that His arms will never tire of holding, of hugging and protecting. And what He knew for me, He knew for each and every one of you.

He knows now – and we can know too – that He will *never* fail us. He is there with us, in our confusion and our pain. He understands all our false, and all our real guilt, and often I can picture Him smiling lovingly at our efforts. Sometimes, when the wind blows through the trees in the garden, I can hear His gentle laugh as He tells me to stop struggling, and just wait with Him – wait, and listen.

He does not always give me understanding – not often, in fact! But He *does* tell me to go on, even though sometimes I don't understand. Stumbling and lost, knowing only that I am His, and He is mine, I trip on stones in the path and often fall. I graze my knees, and get blood on my face. Sometimes – too often – I look back, but He is always there to help me. He encourages me to go on, even though on some days, my head is screwed back looking over my shoulder, to what was. And it *is* possible to walk like that, if Someone else is guiding you on – but it's so very much better to walk with your eyes on the road!

If you remember only one thing from this book, and from my stumbling and often faulty efforts to hang on, whilst my world went mad, then let it be this. God is *always* there – for me, and for you. Not for anything in the world would I have had happen to me all that has happened. But at the same time, not for anything in the world would I lose the closeness to God I feel because of it.

I said at the beginning of this book that I don't have the answers for those of us who follow the road of suffering. I *don't* have the answers – but I do know the guide. I do know that whatever we feel – when we are sure we can't make it, and we feel it's too much and that we simply can't go on, and want to end it all – at all these times, and more, the only thing that makes sense of it for me, are two wounded hands held out towards me, wet with His tears for me – and for you. Proof, if proof were needed, of His ever present, never ending, absolutely unshakeable love.

Let The Summer Come

'Let the summer come, my children –
Let the summer come.

Autumn has gone
And the darkness of winter is passing
Into the light of spring –
Where the air is filled with expectancy –
Where the dawn chorus is a song of hope –
Where the buds are peeping through the earth –
And the chrysallis lies curled and tight –
Hidden – unseen
Waiting to struggle out
Into glorious unfettered flight –
Free and light.

And after spring my children
The nights will run into warmth
And stillness
The light gentle evenings
Where the butterfly's journey ends
On the fragile beauty of the rose –
The rose of peace whose fragrance fills the air
With promises of forever.

The gentle buzzing of the honey bee
Promising sweetness and healing –
The haze and balm of long warm days
Where earth and heaven meet
And dance as one in leaps of joy –
Where the cricket and the dragonfly
Join their gentle sounds in a song
Of praise and wonder.

Where there is time to stop
And smell the beauty of the rose –
Where gently mystery shaped clouds touch

And pass – and passing
Speak, and speak, of God –
Where dewdrops glisten and shine
And tell of the promise
Of all the Father has to give –
Where a ray of sunshine warms and touches
And speaks of a love
Straight from the Father's heart.

The twilight of evening –
The darkness of night –
The golden rays of dawn –
Winter is passing
Into the expectancy of spring.

But let the summer come my children
Let the summer come.'

APPENDIX

Chapter 1 – Page 17

The Benedictine Abbey to which I belong is not an 'active' order. The nuns do not have jobs outside the Abbey walls. They run a guest house for those seeking a place of rest or retreat, but their main calling is to a life of prayer, which is lived within the cloister, so they are called an 'enclosed' Order. They pray, and help us to learn to pray, contemplatively. To pray in this way is to draw aside to a place of quiet and attempt to quieten our hearts and minds. It is simply to be still – to wait and listen. At one and the same time, this is both incredibly simple and profoundly difficult! For what are we waiting and listening? We are waiting for God to work in us and through us, out into the world – we are listening for His still small voice. As Bishop Peter Ball, that modern contemplative monk whom I both respect and admire, said to me one day when we were talking: 'Sue, we can wait four hours for just one glimpse. It's hard, hard work, but when we've been given a glimpse, we long and long for more.' How right he was! I cannot describe in words exactly what those 'glimpses' feel like, except to say that when it happens – you know! It is wonderful and makes the waiting worth every minute. Bishop Peter also said: 'Contemplation is what links earth and heaven together.' When we wait, even though we can't always *feel* it, God *is* working in us, and whatever He does in us we take out into our daily lives – and the world.

To live a contemplative life is not to separate the sacred and the secular, but to see the whole of life as many different ways of prayer. Therefore, if I am cooking a meal for friends, I can consciously say to God: 'I offer the cooking of this meal to You as an offering. Please accept it and use it as You will.' Or when I am looking after a patient at Burrswood, I can say: 'Lord, this person represents You to me. Please help me to treat them with the respect You deserve.' Benedictines say: 'Let each be the first to see Christ in the other.' So even the simplest task can be turned into an offering – a prayer.

The commitment involved is initially that of two and a half years' training – six months as an Oblate 'postulant', followed by another two years as a 'novice'. We are received at the start of this time into the fellowship of Oblates within our particular community in a simple but beautiful service, usually following the Monastic Office of Vespers at 4.45pm. We take a name as an Oblate. I chose St Luke as he is one of my favourite saints, being the patron saint of physicians and artists. As it is a masculine name, I am known as Sister Sue Luke, and eleven years on I still thrill every time I see it written, or hear it said! After our training period, we are received as full Oblates in another beautiful little service. We offer a candle as a sign of our commitment to God through the rule of St Benedict and our fellowship in the wider community. This is then lit and placed on the altar. We try to live a life which is Christ-centred, according to the Rule of St Benedict. (St Benedict was born in AD 480 and died in 543. It is thought he wrote his Rule around 530 whilst at Monte Cassino in Italy). We read this Rule once a year, as it has been translated by one of the nuns into contemporary English.

We promise 'Conversion of life' – to let God work in us and change us – what is called in Latin 'Conversatio Morum'; this has the meaning of not having been converted, but of being continually open to change. The element of stability is important in Benedictine spirituality too – these two things have to be seen together.

One of the early saints, St Gregory of Nyssa, said: 'Stability and movement should be the same thing.' The stability of which we speak is being rooted and grounded in Christ, and held by that stability, firstly in our own community, and at the same time, in the Benedictine community world-wide – a thought which to this day both humbles and excites me.

In practical terms our commitment means working out a 'rule of life' with our Oblate Sister which is realistic for our life. We try to make one retreat a year and also attend special Quiet Days and other events for Oblates at the Abbey. We have our own Office Book – the book which contains six of the sevenfold prayers of the monastic life, which are said at intervals throughout the day. (Oblates' office books do not contain the night office of Vigils.) We are not expected to say all six offices, but work out with our Oblate Sister the best two of three we can say each day. With nursing shifts, mine have to vary daily. This saying of the offices is not a strict disciplinarian rule that we break at our peril, but rather an aid, a helper to draw us back to an awareness of God during the busyness of life. I love to say the office at the same time as the nuns in my community, as then I know that I am joining with my monastic sisters – and indeed with the whole Benedictine community world-wide – in worshipping God. Sometimes it is very hard, and requires much discipline, but it keeps us close both to our Lord and to our sisters in the cloister, giving a wonderful feeling of belonging to both of these.

BIBLIOGRAPHY

Chapter One
1   Rainer Maria Rilke, source untraced. Used with permission of Suhrkamp Verlag, Frankfurt.

Chapter Three
2   David Biebel, *If God Is So Good, Why Do I Hurt So Bad?* (Spire 1959).

Chapter Four
3   Ibid.
4   Ibid.
5   Rob Parsons, *Loving Against The Odds* (Hodder & Stoughton, 1994). Used with permission.

Chapter Six
6   Elizabeth Jennings, *In Christ's Place*. Source untraced. Used with permission of Carcanet Press.

List of Help Agencies

1   The Samaritans
    A nationwide charity, founded in 1953, which exists to provide confidential emotional support to any person, irrespective of race, creed, age or status, who is suicidal or despairing, and to increase public awareness of suicidal feelings. They can be contacted in any of the following ways:
    By phone: 0345 909090 UK single national number, local call rate anywhere in the UK.
    1050 609090 Irish single national number, local call rate anywhere in the Republic.
    Local branch numbers and addresses to be found in telephone directories.
    By E-mail: jo@.samaritans.org
    or samaritans@anon.twwells.com (via an anonymous server)
    By Letter: Chris, The Samaritans, PO Box 9090, Slough, SL1 1UU
    Text Phone: North 01204 531122 (based in Bolton) South 0181 780 2521 (based in Putney).

2   SANELINE
    A national telephone helpline offering accurate up-to-date information and emotional support to people with mental health problems, their carers/families/friends and interested professionals. Information is available on local/national mental health services, medication, illnesses, mental health law and treatments and therapies. Trained volunteers answer the telephone.
    Address: SANELINE, 199–205 Old Marylebone Road, London NW1 5QP

Tel: 0345 678000
Open: 2pm–12 midnight every day of the year (including Christmas and New Year).

3   Families Need Fathers
Established to encourage shared parenting. Their primary aim is to ensure that when parents separate the children are able to maintain a good relationship with both parents.
Tel: 0990 502506; 0181 295 1956; 0171 564 6191 or 01920 462825

4   Broken Rites
A support group founded by former wives of clergymen and can be contacted on 01142 362825, or through your local Diocesan Office or local Archdeacon.

5   Al-Anon
Confidential emotional support to those who are suffering from alcohol dependency, their relatives, partners and friends.
Tel: 0345 697555

6   Relate
A national counselling service helping those who are experiencing marriage breakdown.
Tel: 01788 573241